LET
THERE BE
LIGHT

MICHAEL SCANTLEBURY

LET THERE BE LIGHT
Copyright © 2025 by Michael Scantlebury

Editorial Consultants:
Main Text: Anita Thompson – 604-521-6042 | Question Section: Anoja Wijesuriya

All Scripture quotations, unless otherwise indicated, are taken from the Young Literal Translation (YLT), Revised Standard Version. Copyright © 1946, 1952, and 1971 the Division of Christian Education of the National Council of the Churches of Christ in the United States of America. Used by permission. All rights reserved. All Scriptures marked KJV are taken from the King James Version; all marked NIV are from The New International Version; and those marked MSG are from The Message Bible and is used by permission.

Hebrew and Greek definitions are from James Strong, Strong's Exhaustive Concordance of the Bible (Peabody, MA: Hendrickson Publishers, n.d.).

Michael Scantlebury has taken author's prerogative in capitalizing certain words that are not usually capitalized according to standard grammatical practice. Also, please note that the name satan and related names are not capitalized as we choose not to acknowledge him, even to the point of disregarding standard grammatical practice.

ISBN: Softcover: 978-1-4866-2789-9
eBook ISBN: 978-1-4866-2790-5

Word Alive Press
119 De Baets Street Winnipeg, MB R2J 3R9
www.wordalivepress.ca

WORD ALIVE
—PRESS—

Cataloguing in Publication information is can be obtained from Library and Archives Canada.

Let There Be Light is a serious study on Light and darkness. Dr. Michael is a scholar who has studied this subject to such a depth. That you must stop and think about each statement. I appreciate his gift to study out a matter in such a way, the spiritual background and historical background with spiritual applications.

Wow! this is an evocative book, you will be blessed as you read it. Jesus said He is the Light of the world (John 8:12) and then said you (the Believer) , are the light of the world (Matthew 5:14). Let us continue to study and pray that the Spirit of wisdom and revelation works mightily in us. Then we can shine brightly with the love of Lord Jesus in a dark world.

— Dr. Mark R. Van Gundy, Doctorate in Theology
Revival N Nations, Wales, UK

As ever, Apostle Michael Scantlebury has written a book which is well reasoned, full of Scripture and thought provoking. Michael challenges the strongly held views of many, but bases his thoughts on Scripture, history and biblical interpretation. Michael's writings seek to challenge and encourage us to press deeper into the word of God for clear revelation on topics where it is very easy to go with the status quo.

—Apostle Brian Agnew MBE
Founder of LCC Community Trust, Senior Leader Lisburn City Church

One of the most intriguing elements of our world is light—in all its forms. To speak about it, to explain it, to vigorously debate it, or even to defend it demands more than just definitions and disjointed thoughts. Light infuses light. It's in that direction that Dr. Michael Scantlebury passionately meanders through this book, Let There Be Light, allowing every reader a unique and biblical perspective on the subject. "Let there be Light" offers a deep dive into the design dimension of light as originated by the Father of Light, God Himself. Drawing from the Old and New Testaments, along with a plethora of scholarly historical evidence, we are taken on an exploration grounded in the understanding and representation of that light. The authentic Christian themes that God is light, we are children of the light and not of the night, propose a corrective and instructive stance about the Christians' function as the people of light. Once again, Dr. Scantlebury has insightfully delivered another tool for learning, one that tackles this largely misunderstood Christian thought about the end of the age. This book is compelled to replenish our world with evidence, the conquering power of the Light of the world—Jesus Christ.

—Frampton Paul—Christian Thought Leader,
Potter's Vessel Ministries and Truelife Radio, Brooklyn, New York.

"Let there be light." These are four of the most powerful words ever uttered, spoken by the Creator at the dawn of time as recorded in the book of Genesis. They represent the definitive moment when chaos was ordered back into alignment, potential was unlocked, and creation begun. For too long, many have believed that this command belongs solely to a power outside of ourselves. This book challenges us who are tired of navigating a dimly lit world and are ready to gaze into the divine Light dwelling within every born-again Believer to receive spiritual truth and revelation. The author, Apostle Michael Scantlebury, masterfully presents compelling research and historical facts, arguing that true light—revelation, understanding, clarity, hope, and truth—is not something we passively inherit from theologians, but something we actively seek from the ultimate Source of Light within us.

Get ready to flip the switch of your mind. Your journey from passive observer to active, truth-seeking disciple.

—Siam Chen – Associate Pastor
Gospel Tabernacle – Burnaby, BC

In the Holy Scriptures, the term **"light"** is used frequently, and even in the modern world, it continues to carry deep significance. In this book, as usual, Dr. Michael Scantlebury provides a clear biblical viewpoint on the subject of light and, most importantly, shines **"light"** on Matthew 24.

Matthew 24 has been a subject of gross misinterpretation and misapplication throughout history. Yet, as a skillful, wise master builder with apostolic patience and precision Dr. Michael expounds on Matthew 24, peeling off layers of years of misunderstanding and contextually shedding true light on the chapter.

He employs the same template to uncover depths of truth in the Book of Revelation. With this scholarly work, we no longer approach the book from a place of fear, but from a place of understanding and light.

Paul's prayer for the Believers was that their hearts would be **"flooded with light"** (*Ephesians 1:18, NLT*). I pray that as you read this book, you will be further enlightened concerning the truths inherent in God's Word.

—Maxwell E. Ogaga
Pastoral Overseer, GKAM Network of Churches

It is not often that I read a book in one sitting. Also, I am not one for "End times" teaching as God has kept me from it to be an encourager to Spiritual growth and Kingdom principles. The principles of Spiritual Light are important to me and I was intrigued by the material my friend sent me. I have heard of this teaching from others (such as Dr. Coates) but never read any of it, or to be honest, nor cared to. But since my friend asked me to, I did. I found it fascinating, and truly, if I was in a different place, would have put myself into full investigation mode. So much here, most of it makes sense. After reading, I still want more information on Light because I know there is so much more, but I realize the purpose. The aspects of "end times" leaves me with questions with certain Scriptures not addressed. That is a good thing as it normally would put me in full study mode, but for now, I am emersed in some other projects. I would love for others to read this and have them look outside the box of their past teachings, study, and find the truth for themselves and maybe, just maybe, add their findings. Thank you, my brother, for stretching my thought process. I believe that "Light" might be a thorough study in the near future. Blessings!

—Bishop Daniel H. Elder
Sr. Pastor at Peru Church of God. P.O. Box 7, Lewis, NY 12950

Michael Scantelbury's latest work is a transformative masterpiece that will leave you inspired and equipped with powerful insights. This profound study is a must-read, offering a deep dive into remarkable research and unveiling revelations that will reshape your perspective. Get ready to be challenged and empowered!

—Apostle Ashwyn Lewis
Kingdom Revival Ministries, Cape Town South Africa

Other Books by Michael Scantlebury

The Resurrection of the Dead Ones
Navigating Through Spiritual Transitions
Exploring the Secrets of Hidden Wealth
God's Eternal Plan
Understanding the Both Sides of Faith
Understanding the Revelation – An In-Depth Study
Are We Living in The End Times or The Last Days?
Fathers and Sons – An Unveiling
Heaven and Earth – A Biblical Understanding
My Ponderings
Understanding the Kingdom of God and The Church of Jesus Christ
Eschatology – A Biblical View
As It Was in the Beginning, So Shall It Be...
Daniel In Babylon – The Study Guide
Principles for Victorious Living Volume II
Principles for Victorious Living Volume I
Present Truth Lifestyle – Daniel In Babylon
Esther: Present Truth Church
The Fortress Church
Called to be An Apostle – An Autobiography
Leaven Revealed
Five Pillars of The Apostolic
Apostolic Purity
Apostolic Reformation
Jesus Christ The Apostle and High Priest of Our Profession
Kingdom Advancing Prayer Volume I
Kingdom Advancing Prayer Volume II
Kingdom Advancing Prayer Volume III
Internal Reformation
God's Nature Expressed Through His Names
"I Will Build My Church." – Jesus Christ

CONTENTS

FOREWORD

IT IS A RARE AND INVIGORATING EXPERIENCE TO ENCOUNTER A WORK THAT challenges the very foundations of our long-held beliefs, not to dismantle them, but to invite us into a deeper, more luminous understanding of God's eternal truth. Let There Be Light by Apostle Michael Scantlebury is precisely such a work. This book is not a casual theological read; it is a passionate, scholarly, and spirit-led expedition into the heart of Scripture, beckoning us to see the familiar with revolutionary new eyes.

From its very opening, this book confronts us with a question that many of us have read over countless times without truly seeing: Why was light created on Day One, while the sun, moon, and stars were not fashioned until Day Four? This initial query is the spark that ignites a profound exploration into the nature of God, His Kingdom, and our identity as children of light. Apostle Scantlebury masterfully guides us to understand that the first command, "Let there be light," was the declaration of a spiritual reality—the very essence and power of God Himself—that precedes and supersedes the physical creation that would follow.

What unfolds from this starting point is a sweeping biblical narrative that recontextualizes our place in God's story. Scantlebury argues with compelling scriptural support that the central drama of the Bible—the conflict between light and darkness, the establishment of the New Covenant, and the triumphant coming of Christ in judgment and glory—was decisively and victoriously concluded in the first century. He shines a brilliant and, for some, a challenging light on prophecies in Matthew 24 and the Book of Revelation, presenting a case that these were fulfilled in the events surrounding AD 70, particularly the destruction of the Temple in Jerusalem. This "Preterist" perspective, as it is known, is not presented as a mere academic theory but as the key that unlocks the Bible's own timeline, freeing the Gospel from an endlessly deferred future and anchoring it in a finished, historical victory.

This is not a message of closure, but one of profound commissioning. By demonstrating that the "end" spoken of by Jesus and the Apostles was the end of the Old Covenant age, Apostle Scantlebury liberates the people of God to fully embrace our eternal, "world without end" mandate. We are not a people waiting for a kingdom to come; we are a people called to manifest the unshakable, ever-advancing Kingdom of Light now, having been transferred into it by the finished work of Christ.

Let There Be Light is a clarion call to move out of the shadows of escapist theologies and into the brilliant day for which we were created. It is a call to walk in the understanding, authority, and power of that original. As you turn these pages, prepare to have your assumptions tested, your spirit stirred, and your vision clarified. You are holding an invitation to step more fully into the marvelous light of Christ and to become, as you were always meant to be, a radiant beacon of His glory to the world.

It is my sincere pleasure and honor to commend this significant work to you. May it enlighten your mind, ignite your heart, and empower your walk as a child of the Almighty God.

—Dr. Ali Feizi
Snr Pastor, Gospel Tabernacle, Burnaby, BC

Introduction

Awoke early one morning and I had the following question swirling around in my heart. So here goes: Why was light and darkness created on Day one and the sun and moon on Day four?

Here is what the Scripture says in Genesis 1:1-5

In the beginning God created the heaven and the earth. And the earth was without form, and void; and darkness was upon the face of the deep. And the Spirit of God moved upon the face of the waters. ***And God said, Let there be light: and there was light. And God called the light Day***, and the darkness he called Night. And the evening and the morning were **the first day.** And God saw the light, that it was good: and God divided the light from the darkness.

Then in Genesis 1:14-18 we read the following:

And God said, Let there be lights in the firmament of the heaven to divide the day from the night; and let them be for signs, and for seasons, and for days, and years: and let them be for lights in the firmament of the heaven to give light upon the earth: and it was so. *And God made two great lights; the greater light to rule the day, and the lesser light to rule the night*: he made the stars also.

And God set them in the firmament of the heaven to give light upon the earth, and to rule over the day and over the night, and to divide the light from the darkness: and God saw that it was good. *And the evening and the morning* **were the fourth day**. (Emphasis Author's)

Has anyone reading this book ever thought of why this is?
Then in 1 Thessalonians 5:5-11 [KJV] we read.

Ye are all the children of light, and the children of the day: we are not of the night, nor of darkness. Therefore let us not sleep, as do others; but let us watch and be sober. For they that sleep, sleep in the night; and they that be drunken are drunken in the night. But let us, who are of the day, be sober, putting on the breastplate of faith and love; and for an helmet, the hope of salvation. For God hath not appointed us to wrath, but to obtain salvation by our Lord Jesus Christ, who died for us, that, whether we wake or sleep, we should live together with him. Wherefore comfort yourselves together, and edify one another, even as also ye do.

Then in Matthew 22:13 we read:

Then said the king to the servants, Bind him hand and foot, and take him away, and cast him into outer darkness; there shall be weeping and gnashing of teeth.

I tell you, my spirit man was just pressing for more. Because day and night according to the Scriptures seem to suggest that it is much more than we are led to believe. Because on the 4th day, a greater light was created to rule the day that was created since day 1, so then for me the question becomes—what was that Day like? And the Scripture seems to point to the idea that when we become 'born again' we step into THAT DAY, which was created on Day 1.

As we were in service two days after I sent this book to one of my editors, then our assistant Pastor, Siam Chen from our ministry, ministered a word on this Light that God called forth on the first day. The title of her message was "The Light of Jesus—From Gamma Ray to Glory" and she had no idea that I had just completed a book about this same issue. She used the following passages of Scripture:

John 8:12

Then Jesus spoke to them again, saying, "I am the light of the world. He who follows Me shall not walk in darkness, but have the light of life."

John 1:6-9

There was a man sent from God, whose name was John. This man came for a witness, to bear witness of the Light, that all through him might believe. He was not that Light, but was sent to bear witness of that Light. That was the true Light which gives light to every man coming into the world.

This Light was a Spiritual, unseen light as the physical light was not created until Day four, as we saw earlier in Genesis 1:14-18.

As we are born-again and enter into God's Kingdom we receive this Light and we become just like Jesus as the Light of this world. We need to lighten this world with this Light. We are not to hide our light under the bushes but we need to put it on a lampstand to give light to all who needs it.

Matthew 5:14-16

You are the light of the world. A city that is set on a hill cannot be hidden. Nor do they light a lamp and put it under a basket, but on a lampstand, and it gives light to all who are in the house. Let your light so shine before men, that they may see your good works and glorify your Father in heaven.

In this book, we would be seeking to understand this. We would look at everything concerning 'light' recorded in the Scriptures. Again remember it is the word of God that declared in Proverbs 4:7

Wisdom is the principal thing; Therefore get wisdom. And in all your getting, get understanding.

A brief note about understanding:

DEFINITION AND SCOPE:
Understanding, in the biblical context, refers to the ability to discern, comprehend, and apply knowledge and wisdom in accordance with God's will. It is a spiritual insight that goes beyond mere intellectual knowledge, involving a heart aligned with God's truth and purposes.

BIBLICAL FOUNDATION:
Understanding is frequently mentioned in the Bible as a desirable and God-given attribute. It is often associated with wisdom and knowledge, forming a triad of virtues that are essential for righteous living. Proverbs 2:6 states, *For the LORD gives wisdom; from His mouth come knowledge and understanding.* This verse highlights that true understanding is a divine gift, bestowed by God upon those who seek Him.

OLD TESTAMENT INSIGHTS:
In the Old Testament, understanding is portrayed as a key component of wisdom. The Book of Proverbs, in particular, emphasizes the importance of understanding in leading a life that honors God. Proverbs 3:5-6 advises, *Trust in the LORD with all your heart, and lean not on your own understanding; in all your ways acknowledge Him, and He will make your paths straight.* Here, understanding is contrasted with human reasoning, underscoring the need to rely on divine guidance.

The account of Solomon is a prime example of God granting understanding. In 1 Kings 3:9, Solomon asks God for "an understanding heart to judge Your people and to discern between good and evil." God responds by granting him unparalleled wisdom and understanding, which becomes evident in his judgments and governance.

NEW TESTAMENT PERSPECTIVES:
In the New Testament, understanding is closely linked to spiritual maturity and discernment. The Apostle Paul frequently prays for believers to grow in understanding. In Ephesians 1:17-18, he writes, "I keep asking that the God of our Lord Jesus Christ, the glorious Father, may give you the Spirit of wisdom and revelation, so that you may know Him better. I pray that the eyes of your heart may be enlightened in order that you may know the hope to which He has called you."

Understanding is also essential for interpreting and applying the teachings of Jesus. In the parable of the Sower, Jesus explains that the seed sown on good soil represents those who hear the word and understand it, leading to a fruitful life (Matthew 13:23).

ROLE IN CHRISTIAN LIFE:
For Christians, understanding is vital for discerning God's will and living a life that reflects His character. It involves a deep engagement with Scripture, prayer, and the guidance of the Holy Spirit. Colossians 1:9-10 encourages believers to be "filled with the knowledge of His will in all spiritual wisdom and understanding, so that you may walk in a manner worthy of the Lord."

Understanding also plays a crucial role in community and relationships. It fosters empathy, patience, and unity among believers, as seen in Ephesians 4:2-3, which calls for humility and gentleness, "bearing with one another in love, making every effort to keep the unity of the Spirit through the bond of peace."

CONCLUSION:
Understanding, as depicted in the Bible, is a profound and multifaceted attribute that encompasses spiritual insight, discernment, and the application of God's truth. It is a gift from God that enables believers to navigate life's complexities with wisdom and grace, ultimately leading to a deeper relationship with Him and a more effective witness to the world.

WIKIPEDIA SAYS THIS ABOUT UNDERSTANDING:
It is a cognitive process related to an abstract or physical object, such as a person, situation, or message whereby one is able to use concepts to model that object. Understanding is a relation between the knower and an object of understanding. Understanding implies abilities and dispositions with respect to an object of knowledge that are sufficient to support intelligent behavior.

Understanding is often, though not always, related to learning concepts, and sometimes also the theory or theories associated with those concepts. However, a person may have a good ability to predict the behavior of an object, animal or system—and therefore may, in some sense, understand it—without necessarily being familiar with the concepts or theories associated with that object, animal, or system in their culture. They may have developed their own distinct concepts and theories, which may be equivalent, better or worse than the recognized standard concepts and theories of their culture. Thus, understanding is correlated with the ability to make inferences. (Love this, it is so true).

Now, let us get into this book! In the first chapter we will take another look at the creation of the world/earth on which we all live.

CHAPTER ONE
THE CREATION OF PLANET EARTH

WE GET OUR FIRST RECORD OF THE CREATION OF THE PLANET ON WHICH WE all live in the first book of the Bible, The Genesis. Let us take a truly deep look at the first few verses:

Here is what the Scripture says in Genesis 1:1-5

In the beginning God created the heaven and the earth. And the earth was without form, and void; and darkness was upon the face of the deep. And the Spirit of God moved upon the face of the waters. And God said, Let there be light: and there was light. And God called the light Day, and the darkness he called Night. *And the evening and the morning* <u>were the first day</u>*. And God saw the light, that it was good: and God divided the light from the darkness.* (Emphasis Author's)

Then in Genesis 1:14-18 we read the following:

And God said, Let there be lights in the firmament of the heaven to divide the day from the night; and let them be for signs, and for seasons, and for days, and years: and let them be for lights in the firmament of the heaven to give light upon the earth: and it was so. <u>And God made two great lights; the greater light to rule the day, and the lesser light to rule the night</u>*: He made the stars also.*

And God set them in the firmament of the heaven to give light upon the earth, and to rule over the day and over the night, and to divide the light from the darkness: and God saw that it was good. <u>*And the evening and the morning were the fourth day*</u>. (Emphasis Author's)

Here we read in the recorded word of God, that God created Light on day one. However, we also read in Genesis 1:16 that He created a greater light to rule over the day He created on day one. The question I had, was what was that Light like, that He called forth on day one?

I believe a point that we need to consider in seeking to answer that question is this: God is Light and in Him there is no darkness and that lucifer was cast out of Heaven before God began to establish earth as a headquarters for the humans [initially Adam and Eve] He was going to create there, and that lucifer in making his new home earth, brought his darkness with him. We know that something happened between Genesis 1:1 and Genesis 1:2, here is what it says:

Genesis 1:1

In the beginning God created the heavens and the earth.

Genesis 1:2

The earth was without form, and void; and darkness was on the face of the deep. And the Spirit of God was hovering over the face of the waters.

In verse one God created the Heavens and the earth, and I submit to you that it was somewhere before verse two that God cast lucifer out of Heaven for his rebellion. When lucifer was cast out of Heaven, I submit to you that he lost any light he would have had and was now consumed by total darkness. And because of that, when God decided it was the time for His brilliant plan to create mankind to deal with lucifer had come, He encountered such chaos and darkness upon the earth that He, the God Who is Light had created and would have had elements of His Light on it, because He cast lucifer and his host of rebellious angels down to earth and they corrupted that Light, now the earth was covered in their darkness. So the first thing that God did was to reestablish His Order to the earth realm before creating the perfect Adam and Eve to deal with lucifer's rebellion.

This therefore leads me to the understanding that lucifer was never intended to be our problem. We were supposed to conquer him and his entire demonic realm and establish God's Kingdom rule over the entire earth realm. To dispossess them and live for the King and His Kingdom.

At creation Adam and Eve the first man and woman had both the Heavenly and earthly in them, when God breathed into Adam a divine body of revelation [which was passed on to Eve through a rib being taken from Adam to form her] so that they did not have to be subjected to any form of training or learning but instinctively just knew. Because we all know that the first couple, Adam and Eve never had to be subjected to any form of learning as we do today. No, they were given a body of knowledge in that breath from the Spirit of God and instinctively just knew. They became God-like in their abilities. And in that act, I believe that God had made them **vice regents** [persons who rule or reign: **LIKE GOVERNORS**] with Him. Their main task was to govern the earth as a territory of Heaven on earth. And we all know that they failed miserably in that undertaking. That when lucifer and his angels were cast down to the earth realm as part punishment for rebelling against their Creator, God Almighty, that they set out to corrupt mankind, thereby causing them to lose that responsibility of assuming the rulership of the earth leading to them enforcing their incorrect understanding of heavenly rule. After all, lucifer wanted to be like God; but we all know that he just could not and would never be able to. He has been completely defeated by the King of kings and Lord of lords, King Jesus.

Now from this we realize that satan was never going to be our problem. Afterall he was cast down to the earth that God had previously created before even creating Adam and Eve. So, they met satan already living on planet earth before them bringing us to understand that they would have had to deal with him in their lives. And in dealing with him they eventually submitted to his cunning.

I do believe that it is the same for us the born-again Believer in Jesus Christ as we seek to extend His Kingdom rule all over planet earth. This was always going to be the situation for all eternity had Adam and Eve not sinned in submitting to the devil's scheme. So please get used to it, satan is here and we need to be able to overcome him. And there is just so much promise to those who **overcome**. Here are a few promises:

Revelation 3:5

He that overcometh, the same shall be clothed in white raiment; and I will not blot out his name out of the book of life, but I will confess his name before my Father, and before his angels.

Revelation 3:12

Him that overcometh will I make a pillar in the temple of my God, and he shall go no more out: and I will write upon him the name of my God, and the name of the city of my God, which is new Jerusalem, which cometh down out of heaven from my God: and I will write upon him my new name.

Revelation 3:21

To him that overcometh will I grant to sit with me in my throne, even as I also overcame, and sat down with My Father on His throne.

In our next chapter we will be exploring the idea 'God is Light'.

Let's assess our understanding of Chapter One: The Creation of Planet Earth

1. What happened on Day 1 of God's creation of planet earth as recorded in Genesis 1?
2. When did God separate the light from the darkness?
3. What are the two great lights that God created to rule the day and night?
4. Do you then agree that light existed before the Sun was created?
5. When did God decide to set the Sun and the Moon to rule over the Day and the Night?
6. What could have happened between the time God Created the heavens and the earth to the time He found it without form and void, darkness engulfing the entire creation?

7. Why did God have to re-establish His Order on earth before creating the perfect humans (Adam and Eve}?
8. According to the author "At creation Adam and Eve had both the Heavenly and Earthly in them"—Are you in agreement with this statement? Why?
9. What could have been the purpose for the first man and woman to have been given the capacity to discern things (God-like ability) from the very beginning?
10. What therefore could have been God's intent for the human race upon planet earth?

CHAPTER TWO
GOD IS LIGHT

1 JOHN 1:5

This is the message which we have heard from Him and declare to you, that God is light and in Him is no darkness at all. [Emphasis Author's]

Now this is the reason why I believe that lucifer had to be cast out of Heaven between Genesis 1:1 and Genesis 1:2 as the earth that God who is light created and would have had to have had dimensions of that light as everything He created was recorded as being very good. However, this is the place we see dissatisfaction with what God saw, as the earth was void and without form and darkness covered it. I submit that lucifer the prince of darkness caused that and the God who is LIGHT came and corrected that situation.

While there is no passage in the Scriptures that says specifically that lucifer dwells in darkness, there is an article on Wikipedia, that I would love to cite here:

The Prince of Darkness is a term used in John Milton›s poem *Paradise Lost* referring to satan as the embodiment of evil. It is an English translation of the Latin phrase *princeps tenebrarum*, which occurs in the *Acts of Pilate*, written in the 4th Century, in the *Historia Francorum* by Gregory of Tours (6th Century), in the 11th-Century hymn *Rhythmus de* *die mortis* by Pietro Damiani, and in a sermon by *Bernard of Clairvaux* from the 12th Century.

Light is used to symbolize God, faith, and holiness throughout Scripture. As Christians, we are called to not only walk in the light but to be the light for others. Let us view a few Scriptural references to God as LIGHT and let us review these Bible verses to gain a better understanding and interpretation of the positive notion light has in the Bible.

In Matthew 4 we read about Jesus' time to step into public ministry and before doing that He did the following:

Matthew 4:1

Then Jesus was led up by the Spirit into the wilderness to be tempted by the devil.

Then in verse 16 we read about Jesus' entry into public ministry:

Matthew 4:16

The people who sat in darkness have seen a great light, *And upon those who sat in the region and shadow of death* Light has dawned. (Emphasis Author's)

We read the record of Jesus' first miracle on someone in His public ministry:

John 9:1-5

Now as Jesus passed by, He saw a man who was blind from birth. And His disciples asked Him, saying, "Rabbi, who sinned, this man or his parents, that he was born blind?" Jesus answered, "Neither this man nor his parents sinned, but that the works of God should be revealed in him. I must work the works of Him who sent Me while it is day; the night is coming when no one can work. As long as I am in the world, I am the light of the world." (Emphasis Author's)

John 8:12

Then Jesus spoke to them again, saying, "I am the light of the world. He who follows Me shall not walk in darkness, but have the light of life." (Emphasis Author's)

1 John 1:5-9

This is the message which we have heard from Him and declare to you, that God is light and in Him is no darkness at all. If we say that we have fellowship with Him, and walk in darkness, we lie and do not practice the truth. But if we walk in the light as He is in the light, we have fellowship with one another, and the blood of Jesus Christ His Son cleanses us from all sin. If we say that we have no sin, we deceive ourselves, and the truth is not in us. If we confess our sins, He is faithful and just to forgive us our sins and to cleanse us from all unrighteousness. (Emphasis Author's)

So, from these few passages we can see that the Scriptures declare that God is indeed LIGHT and in Him there is absolutely no darkness.

Please understand this: there are two kingdoms operating in this world; the Kingdom of God and the kingdom of darkness. Note the contrast in the following chart:

LET US BRIEFLY CONTRAST THESE TWO KINGDOMS

THE KINGDOM OF GOD	THE KINGDOM OF DARKNESS
Light	Darkness
Understanding	Ignorance
Life	Death
Righteousness	Unrighteousness; iniquity; lawlessness
Peace	Turmoil; unrest; anxiety
Joy	Sorrow; mourning

Those who know Jesus as Lord have been brought OUT of their darkness and into His marvellous LIGHT. We have passed from death unto life…

Another thing that we need to understand is the fact that the devil in the kingdom of darkness rules **by** ignorance—not "**in ignorance**" but by it; he rules his subjects by keeping them in ignorance of the true nature of things and the fact there is the existence of God's Kingdom, which they could gain access to through the finished work of Jesus Christ. The Apostle Paul declared—2 Corinthians 4:3-4

But also if our gospel is hidden, it is hidden to those being lost, in whom the god of this world has blinded the minds of the unbelieving ones, so that the light of the glorious gospel of Christ (who is the image of God) should not dawn on them.

Now let us explore a few passages that show that when we are born-again in Jesus we too must walk in the light as He is in the light:

There's a presence of God in those who walk in the light. They aren't always aware of the light—but it's evident in how they speak, act, and think about life, work, family, and the Christian faith. The light that is within all Believers exposes and drives out the darkness. satan and his demons can't stand the light of Jesus Christ in His people. What can we learn from the 7 great Bible verses about walking in the light? Here they are:

WALK IN THE LIGHT OF JESUS SO YOU DON'T STUMBLE:
Psalm 56:13

For You have delivered my soul from death. Have You not kept my feet from falling, That I may walk before God In the light of the living?

When we walk in the light of Jesus Christ, we don't stumble in sinful choices. We are compelled by the light to recognize and resist the temptations of the flesh. Our decisions to walk away or to walk towards sins will have an effect on the brightness of the light in our lives.

WALK IN THE LIGHT OF JESUS SO YOU COULD ENJOY THE RICHES OF HIS GLORY:
Psalm 89:15

Blessed are the people who know the joyful sound! They walk, O LORD, in the light of Your countenance.

Being in the light of Jesus Christ reveals the favour of God in our daily walk. The blessing of the light is so much more than material things; rather it's the Lord's presence and peace that hovers over us at home, work, play and community. It is always with us as Believers in Christ.

WALK IN THE LIGHT OF CHRIST AS YOUR SPIRITUAL BIRTHRIGHT:
Isaiah 2:5

O house of Jacob, come and let us walk In the light of the LORD.

The light of Jesus Christ is a birthright to those who are the children of Abraham through the Covenant. We are the stars in the sky and the sand by the seashore that represented Abraham's seed through Isaac. Our spiritual heritage leads every Believer down the path of victory over sin and death. We are no longer slaves and captives—we are free to accomplish everything that God has called us to complete.

WALK IN THE LIGHT INSTEAD OF DARKNESS SO YOU COULD HAVE THE HOPE OF ETERNAL LIFE:
Isaiah 9:2

The people who walked in darkness Have seen a great light; Those who dwelt in the land of the shadow of death, Upon them a light has shined.

Many of us can remember that moment of turning from darkness to the light. In our sinfulness the darkness was normal and we accepted it as a part of our lives. However because our hearts were ready—the light wasn't a piercing pain in our spiritual eyes—rather it was a warm and welcoming light of hope.

WALK IN THE LIGHT OF JESUS AFTER YOU ARE BORN-AGAIN SO YOU COULD HAVE DIRECTION AND PURPOSE:
John 8:12

Then Jesus spoke to them again, saying, "I am the light of the world. He who follows Me shall not walk in darkness, but have the light of life." (Emphasis Author's)

In this generation, many call themselves the "light", but they are counterfeits and cause many people to fall away from God. The light of Jesus Christ doesn't make excuse our sins, but instead His sacrifice brings us to a place of repentance with a desire to change the course. Jesus will always lead us in the right direction for God's purpose, ALWAYS!

WALK IN THE LIGHT OF JESUS AS CHILDREN OF THE LIGHT SO YOUR STEPS MAY NOT FAULTER:
John 12:35-36

> *Then Jesus said to them,* "A little while longer the light is with you. Walk while you have the light, lest darkness overtake you; he who walks in darkness does not know where he is going. While you have the light, believe in the light, that you may become sons of light." *These things Jesus spoke, and departed, and was hidden from them.* (Emphasis Author's)

As children of the light, we obey the precepts of our Heavenly Father and resist the temptation to disobey. We are the children of light when we obey what the Bible teaches and walk in faith. By following the light, we move in the right direction even though we can't always see the next steps.

WALK IN THE LIGHT OF JESUS AS FELLOW BELIEVERS IN ORDER TO HAVE RIGHT RELATIONSHIPS WITH OTHERS:
1 John 1:7

> *But if we walk in the light as He is in the light, we have fellowship with one another, and the blood of Jesus Christ His Son cleanses us from all sin.*

Constant conflict, backbiting, and strife can't survive in the light. Only those who consistently walk in the light of Christ can enjoy fruitful and loving relationships. The fellowship and love that we have for the people of God is revealed as the light shines from within. We no longer stay committed to an unforgiving nor unloving attitude because the light won't tolerate it.

WALKING IN THE LIGHT
To walk in the light is to have a daily commitment to living out a righteous life. Those who are compelled to walk in the light resist fellowship with

the darkness of the devil, demons, the world, or the flesh. Walking in the light renews and refreshes us within so that we are empowered to be a refreshment to those around us.

The phrase *let there be light* is a translation of the Hebrew phrase *yehi 'or*, which was translated *"fiat lux"* in Latin. A literal translation would be a command, something like "Light, exist." God is speaking into the void and commanding light to come into being. The Bible tells us that God created the Heavens and the earth and everything else that exists by simply speaking them into existence (Genesis 1). His personality, power, creativity, and beauty were expressed in creation the same way an artist's personality and personal attributes are expressed through art or music. The idea of light, existing first in God's mind, was given form by the words "Let there be light" or "Let light exist."

The reality of the creative power of God's voice has important spiritual implications that go well beyond the creation account itself. Light is often used as a metaphor in the Bible, and the word *illumination* ("divine enlightenment of the human heart with truth") has to do with bringing things into the light. Spiritual illumination is a kind of "creation" that occurs in a human heart. *"God, who said, 'Let light shine out of darkness,' made His light shine in our hearts to give us the light of the knowledge of God's glory displayed in the face of Christ"* (2 Corinthians 4:6—*For it is the God who commanded light to shine out of darkness, who has shone in our hearts to give the light of the knowledge of the glory of God in the face of Jesus Christ.*). Jesus Himself is "the light of the world" (John 8:12—*Then Jesus spoke to them again, saying, "I am the light of the world. He who follows Me shall not walk in darkness, but have the light of life."*).

When God said, *"Let there be light,"* at the creation, and light appeared, it showed God's creative power and absolute control. The physical light that God made on the first day of creation is a wonderful picture of what He does in every heart that trusts in Christ, the True Light. There is no need to walk in the darkness of sin and death; in Christ, we *"will never walk in darkness, but will have the light of life"* (John 8:12).

In our next chapter we will be looking at 'The Power of Light.'

Let's assess our understanding of Chapter Two: God Is Light

1. According to the author, the reason for darkness and void upon the earth when God hovered over the earth in Genesis 1:2, was most

likely because of lucifer and his angels who were cast down from Heaven, caused it to be so. Do you consider this to be a possibility? If not Why?

3. What are some of the Scriptures that use Light as a symbol of God, faith and holiness?
4. What are the two kingdoms that operate upon this earth?
5. How will you distinguish between these two kingdoms?
6. Expound on the statement: "the devil in the kingdom of darkness rules by ignorance—not in ignorance"
7. Why is it necessary for us to walk in the light when we are born again and accept Jesus as our Savior?
8. What are the 7 bible verses that talk about walking in the light? Briefly explain in your own words what the scripture is talking about and how it applies to us today?
9. As a born-again child of God, how can others benefit from your commitment to walking in His light daily?
10. How is the Hebrew phrase 'yehi' translated into English?
11. The author's statement: "The idea of light, existing first in God's mind, was given form by the words "Let there be light" or "Let light exist". How do you feel about this statement?
12. Do you agree that Spiritual illumination is a kind of "creation" that occurs in the human heart? Explain
13. What is the relationship between God calling forth light into being and what He does in the hearts of those who trust Christ?

CHAPTER THREE
THE POWER OF LIGHT

Proverbs 4:7 declares:

Wisdom is the principal thing; Therefore get wisdom. And in all your getting, get understanding.

The word understanding carries the understanding of light. It is similar to someone saying 'is like a light went on' when I understood what you said.

In the biblical context, understanding refers to the ability to discern, comprehend, and apply knowledge and wisdom in accordance with God's will. It goes beyond mere intellectual knowledge, involving a heart aligned with God's truth and purposes. Understanding allows individuals to perceive deeper spiritual truths and make wise decisions that reflect God's teachings. It is considered a gift from God that enables Believers to gain wisdom and insight through the proper application of God's truth. Understanding is also associated with wisdom and discernment, enriching the spiritual journey of Christians.

DEFINITION AND SCOPE OF UNDERSTANDING:
Understanding, in the biblical context, refers to the ability to discern, comprehend, and apply knowledge and wisdom in accordance with God's

will. It is a spiritual insight that goes beyond mere intellectual knowledge, involving a heart aligned with God's truth and purposes.

Matthew 11:25

> *At that time Jesus answered and said,* "I thank You, Father, Lord of heaven and earth, that You have hidden these things from the wise and prudent and have revealed them to babes. (Emphasis Author's)

BIBLICAL FOUNDATION:

Understanding is frequently mentioned in the Bible as a desirable and God-given attribute. It is often associated with wisdom and knowledge, forming a triad of virtues that are essential for righteous living. Proverbs 2:6 states, «*For the LORD gives wisdom; from His mouth come knowledge and understanding.*" This verse highlights that true understanding is a divine gift, bestowed by God upon those who seek Him.

OLD TESTAMENT INSIGHTS:

In the Old Testament, understanding is portrayed as a key component of wisdom literature. The Book of Proverbs, in particular, emphasizes the importance of understanding in leading a life that honors God. Proverbs 3:5-6 advises, «*Trust in the LORD with all your heart, and lean not on your own understanding; in all your ways acknowledge Him, and He will make your paths straight.*" Here, understanding is contrasted with human reasoning, underscoring the need to rely on divine guidance.

The account of Solomon is a prime example of God granting understanding. In 1 Kings 3:9, Solomon asks God for "*an understanding heart to judge Your people and to discern between good and evil.*" God responds by granting him unparalleled wisdom and understanding, which becomes evident in his judgments and governance.

NEW TESTAMENT PERSPECTIVES:

In the New Testament, understanding is closely linked to spiritual maturity and discernment. The Apostle Paul frequently prays for believers to grow in understanding. In Ephesians 1:17-18, he writes, "*I keep asking that the God of our Lord Jesus Christ, the glorious Father, may give you the Spirit of wisdom and revelation, so that you may know Him better. I pray that the eyes of your heart may be enlightened in order that you may know the hope to which He has called you."*

Understanding is also essential for interpreting and applying the teachings of Jesus. In the parable of the Sower, Jesus explains that the seed sown on good soil represents those who hear the word and understand it, leading to a fruitful life (Matthew 13:23).

ROLE IN CHRISTIAN LIFE:
For Christians, understanding is vital for discerning God's will and living a life that reflects His character. It involves a deep engagement with Scripture, prayer, and the guidance of the Holy Spirit. Colossians 1:9-10 encourages Believers to be *"filled with the knowledge of His will in all spiritual wisdom and understanding, so that you may walk in a manner worthy of the Lord."*

Understanding also plays a crucial role in community and relationships. It fosters empathy, patience, and unity among believers, as seen in Ephesians 4:2-3, which calls for humility and gentleness, *"bearing with one another in love, making every effort to keep the unity of the Spirit through the bond of peace."*

CONCLUSION:
Understanding, as depicted in the Bible, is a profound and multifaceted attribute that encompasses spiritual insight, discernment, and the application of God's truth. It is a gift from God that enables Believers to navigate life's complexities with wisdom and grace, ultimately leading to a deeper relationship with Him and a more effective witness to the world.

Next we will be shinning the Light on Matthew 24.

Let's assess our understanding of Chapter Three: The Power Of Light

1. How is "understanding" defined from a Biblical standpoint?
2. What is the benefit for an individual to gain understanding?
3. Why is "understanding" so important in a Believer's life?
4. Where can a Believer turn to in-order to obtain wisdom as Proverbs 4:7 admonishes all Christians to do?
5. Explain in your own words how Proverbs 2:6 applies to your own life?

6. Why is it not a good idea to depend on human reasoning according to Proverbs 3:5-6?
7. In establishing His government upon the earth (called to be ambassadors for Jesus Christ), why is the gift of Understanding so important?
8. Which Scripture speaks to the importance of understanding for purposes of interpreting and applying the teachings of Jesus?
9. How does understanding impact in building community and maintaining relationships?
10. Do you agree with the author that "understanding" is a profound and multifaceted attribute which ultimately leads a Believer to a deeper relationship with God? Explain.

CHAPTER FOUR
SHINING THE LIGHT ON MATTHEW 24 - I

FOR EXAMPLE MATTHEW 24:14 STATES:

And this gospel of the kingdom will be preached in all the world as a witness to all the nations, and then the end will come.

Now how we interpret this passage makes all the difference. If we are of the mindset that this passage is referring to the entire globe, we would believe that this passage has not been fulfilled. However, if we understand this passage from a first Century mindset everything changes, and here is why.

In the first Century when this prophecy was given the then 'world' was only the following nations:

[1]NATIONS OF THE KNOWN EARTH IN THE FIRST CENTURY:

The first Century of the Common Era (CE) was marked by the dominance of several powerful nations across the known world. Here are some of the key nations that existed during this period:

---

[1] **World map 1 AD - World History Maps:** The DK Atlas of World History, 2000 Edition. Map of "The World in 1 CE". (Pgs 42-43) John Nelson. Interactive Historical Atlas of the World since 500BCE. Map of "Countries of the W... https://www.worldhistorymaps.info › ancient

- **Roman Empire:** The Roman Empire continued to expand its territory and influence, maintain a period of relative stability known as Pax Romana.
- **Han China**: The Western Han dynasty was overthrown by the Xin dynasty in 9 AD, which was then replaced by the Eastern Han dynasty in 25 AD.
- **Parthian Persia**: The Parthian Empire was a significant power in West Asia, known for its military prowess and cultural achievements.
- **Babylonian Empire**: The Babylonian Empire, known for its advanced civilization and military, was a major power in the region.
- **Sasanian Empire**: The Sasanian Empire was another significant power in the Middle East, known for its military and cultural contributions.

These nations played crucial roles in the political and cultural landscape of the first Century CE, influencing the course of history and the development of various societies.[2]

So, if we are to follow Jesus' prophecy to His first Century audience we would realize from historical records that this prophecy was fulfilled in AD 70 with the destruction of the then Jewish temple.

However, this prophecy cannot be taken to mean us in the twenty first Century preaching the Gospel to the whole twenty first Century world. And yes, we could understand and believe that this prophecy was fulfilled in the first Century but the preaching of the Gospel to our world is still very relevant. What I am not saying is that with the fulfillment of that prophecy to the first Century in AD 70 means that preaching of the Gospel was to also cease. NO, absolutely NOT! The Gospel was still preached after AD 70 until this day in the twenty first Century and would continue until...

Here is another thought: Isaiah 45:17

But Israel shall be saved in the LORD with an everlasting salvation: ye shall not be ashamed nor confounded world without end. KJV (Emphasis Author's)

---

[2] **List of political entities in the 1st century - Wikipedia:** This is a list of political entities that existed between 1 AD and 100 AD. Moche-Trujillo. ^ "Maps of the Roman World in the First Century C.E." www.centuryone.com. Retrieved 2024-...https://en.wikipedia.org › wiki

Israel hath been saved in Jehovah, A salvation age-during! Ye are not ashamed nor confounded Unto the ages of eternity! YLT (Emphasis Author's)

Ephesians 3:21

Unto him be glory in the church by Christ Jesus throughout all ages, world without end. Amen. KJV (Emphasis Author's)

to Him be glory in the church by Christ Jesus to all generations, forever and ever. Amen. NKJV (Emphasis Author's)

to Him [is] the glory in the assembly in Christ Jesus, to all the generations of the age of the ages. Amen. YLT (Emphasis Author's)

From these passages we could conclude that this world created by Almighty God was created to last forever. And that when the Scriptures speak about the "end" it is not referring to the end of the world, but the end of the Old Covenant system and the Temple—BIG DIFFERENCE!

WORLD WITHOUT END:
The original meaning of the word "world" in Ephesians 3:21 is often interpreted as **"world without end"** or **"age of ages."** This phrase emphasizes the eternal nature of God's glory and praise, indicating that it will continue throughout all generations and time.

This is one of the most difficult things to grasp for so many in the Body of Christ. That the Bible was given to a first Century audience, living in a first Century world and that it has been mostly fulfilled. And that should not allow us to think that everything is over. That our world has not come to an end, so we need to work with this concept that this world in which we live will eventually have to come to an end, because that is what the prophecies of Scripture was referring to. For most this gives their lives meaning and significance and as such they have **nothing** to live for or to accomplish. Again, let me reiterate this: The **"end"** spoken of in the Scriptures was not referring to the end of time or the world, but was referring to the end of the Old Covenant system and the destruction of the Temple! And we know that this occurred in circa AD 70, and from that time until now the Gospel has been preached and would continue to be preached everywhere.

Not only that but the New Covenant is the final, everlasting covenant and that there is no other covenant to come. It has been finished! This New Covenant that was given to us is an eternal, never ending covenant, unlike the Old Covenant, which ended. I would say **PLAIN and SIMPLE!**

In our next chapter we will be concluding our shinning of the light on Matthew 24!

Let's assess our understanding of Chapter Four: Shining The Light On Matthew 24 - I

1. According to historical records, what was considered the whole world in the 1st Century?
2. Do you agree that the Prophesy in Matthew 24:14 is not referring to us today preaching the Gospel to the whole of the world in the 21st Century?
3. What are your thoughts on Isaiah 45:17 and Ephesians 3:21?
4. Are we to expect an end to the world? Explain
5. Did Jesus say that the New Covenant that He was entering into with His people was to be an Everlasting Covenant? Explain with Scriptural reference.

CHAPTER FIVE
SHINING THE LIGHT ON MATTHEW 24 - II

HAVE YOU EVER CONSIDERED THAT THE PROPHECIES OF JESUS LISTED IN Matthew 24 were fulfilled exactly like He prophesied and can be proven from the Scriptures. Proving that they were not to be fulfilled in our day. Let us briefly review them:

[3]Let Us Examine Verse-By-Verse Matthew 24:4-28!

Matthew 24:4-5

And Jesus answered and said to them: "Take heed that no one deceives you. For many will come in My name, saying, 'I am the Christ,' and will deceive many."

Christians who have heard only the futurist view immediately place these Words of Jesus in the future, shortly before the end of the world.

They are looking for some evil leader or several leaders to start claiming that they are the Christ.

That is the first error we need to correct. Jesus was answering the question concerning when Jerusalem and the Temple would be destroyed.

That event happened in A.D. 70, within 40 years of the time in which Jesus prophesied it. Jesus told His Disciples that soon many people would

---

3 For more on this subject, please see my book "Are We Living In The End-Times or Last Days". Get it here: https://www.amazon.ca/Are-Living-Times-Final-Days/dp/1486623174 or the eBook here: https://apostlemscantlebury.com/store/eschatology-a-biblical-view

come claiming to be the Christ. For Jesus' Words to be fulfilled, those imposters would have had to come in the First Century of the Church.

Did That Happen Historically?

Yes! Right after the death of Jesus, many leaders arose capturing the hearts of the Jewish people. That may seem difficult for us to understand today, but we need to keep in mind the culture of that day. The Jewish people were desperately looking for a Messiah—someone to free them from Roman domination. Their hope and much of their religious system was based on a coming Messiah. When Jesus died, many of His followers gave up believing that He was the Messiah. Other leaders quickly arose, drawing to themselves large followings! For example we could see the following passage, where Apostle Peter warned the Church in the first Century: 2 Peter 2:1

> *But there were also false prophets among the people, even as there will be false teachers among you, who will secretly bring in destructive heresies, even denying the Lord who bought them, and bring on themselves swift destruction.*

The Records of Some of The Early Church Fathers: State: (Eusebius of Caesarea (AD 263–339) was a Roman historian.)

After the Lord was taken up into heaven the demons put forth a number of men who claimed to be gods.[4]

The Venerable Bede (673-735—also known as Saint Bede)

For many came forward, when destruction was hanging over Jerusalem, saying that they were Christs.[5]

John Wesley (1703-1791)

And indeed, never did so many imposters appear in the world as a few years before the destruction of Jerusalem, undoubtedly because that was the time wherein the Jews in general expected the Messiah.[6]

Charles Spurgeon (1834-1892)

A large number of imposters came forward before the destruction of Jerusalem, giving out that they were the anointed of God.[7]

---

[4] Sacred Cows Volume 1 Tipping over Religious Ideas by Pastor Chris Bobblett pg 61
[5] Cited in Thomas Aquinas' Golden Chain, 1956. The Aesthetics of Thomas Aquila's by Umberto Eco published by Harvard University Press
[6] John Wesley's Explanatory Notes https://www.christianity.com/bible/commentary.php?com=wes&b=40&c=24 © 2020 Christianity.com.
[7] The Gospel of the Kingdom: An Exposition of the Gospel of Matthew GLH Publishing, Louisville, KY, p. 213

Matthew 24:6-7 Wars and Rumours of Wars!

And you will hear of wars and rumours of wars. See that you are not troubled; for all these things must come to pass, but the end is not yet. For nation will rise against nation, and kingdom against kingdom. And there will be famines, pestilences, and earthquakes in various places.

Approximately 2,000 years ago when Jesus was sitting on the Mount of Olives with His disciples, He prophesied of coming wars. Interestingly, there were no signs of "wars and rumours of wars" when Jesus prophesied this. The power of Rome seemed to be stable, strong, irresistible, and permanent. Historically, the period was referred to as Pax Romana, that is, "Roman Peace." Of course, the enemies of Rome would not have spoken of the time so graciously, but Rome definitely was established in that region of the world. It was at that time that Jesus prophesied of coming wars.

Did The Prophecy of Jesus Come True Within That Generation?

Indeed! Wars began to break out all over the empire. The Jews lived in constant fear, with 50,000 Jews being slain in Seleucia and 20,000 in Caesarea. Then in A.D. 66, 50,000 Jews were killed in Alexandria. Within a period of 18 months, four emperors in Rome were murdered violently. Civil war broke out in the city of Rome. It was a time of great turmoil, and there were constant rumours of new rebellions.

Matthew 24:7 Famines

For nation will rise against nation, and kingdom against kingdom. And there will be famines, pestilences, and earthquakes in various places.

Did Famines Occur During the Generation of The Disciples?
Let's look at Acts 11 where we are told about a GREAT FAMINE...
Acts 11:27-30 NIV

And in these days prophets came from Jerusalem to Antioch. Then one of them, named Agabus, stood up and showed by the Spirit that there was going to be a great famine throughout all the world, which also happened in the days of Claudius Caesar. Then the disciples, each according to his ability, determined to send relief to the brethren dwelling in Judea. This they also did, and sent it to the elders by the hands of Barnabas and Saul.

That famine was so severe in the region of Judah that we can read two places in the New Testament where Christians took offerings to collect money for Believers suffering there: Acts 11:29-30 and 1 Corinthians 16:1-20.

Acts 11:29-30

Then the disciples, each according to his ability, determined to send relief to the brethren dwelling in Judea. This they also did, and sent it to the elders by the hands of Barnabas and Saul.

1 Corinthians 16:1-4

Now concerning the collection for the saints, as I have given orders to the churches of Galatia, so you must do also: On the first day of the week let each one of you lay something aside, storing up as he may prosper, that there be no collections when I come. And when I come, whomever you approve by your letters I will send to bear your gift to Jerusalem. But if it is fitting that I go also, they will go with me.

The Historian Josephus Wrote About the Devastation of That Period:
But the famine was too hard for all other passions, and it is destructive to nothing so much as to modesty... insomuch that children pulled the very morsels that their fathers were eating out of their very mouths, and what was still more to be pitied, so did the mothers do as to their infants; and when those that were most dear were perishing under their hands, they were not ashamed to take from them the very last drops that might preserve their lives... but the seditions everywhere came upon them immediately and snatched away from them what they had gotten from others, for when they saw any house shut up, this was to them a signal that the people within had gotten some food: whereupon they broke open the doors, and ran in and took pieces of what they were eating, almost up out

of their very throats, and this by force; the old men, who held their food fast, were beaten; and if the women hid what they had within their hands, their hair was torn for so doing; nor was there any commiseration shown either to the aged or to the infants, but they lifted up children from the ground as they hung upon the morsels they had gotten, and shook them down upon the floor.[8]

Knowing about this famine and the destruction of Jerusalem to follow, Jesus said to the women of Jerusalem: in Luke 23:27-29

And a great multitude of the people followed Him, and women who also mourned and lamented Him. But Jesus, turning to them, said, "Daughters of Jerusalem, do not weep for Me, but weep for yourselves and for your children. For indeed the days are coming in which they will say, 'Blessed are the barren, wombs that never bore, and breasts which never nursed!"

Eusebius
Under [Claudius] the world was visited with a famine, which writers that are entire strangers to our religion have recorded in their histories.[9] (Ecclesiastical History, II:8)
Verse 7 Earthquakes in Various Places.

- Not only did the earth quake when Jesus died on the Cross (Matthew 27:51-52)!
It also quaked again when He rose from the dead (Matthew 28:2)
- Not only then but also history tells us that the few years just prior to the fall of Jerusalem in AD70 was a time of unusual seismic activity.
- The most famous was the destruction of Pompeii (a Roman city/town) in AD63.
- Several writers of the period also tell us about earthquakes at Crete, Smyrna, Miletus, Chios, Samos, Laodicea (AD60), Hierapolis (AD60), Campania, Colossae (AD60), Rome and Judea (AD65, 68, 69) ...

[8] The Genuine Works of Flavian Josephus the Jewish Historian Translated from the Original Greek, according to Havercamp's accurate Edition. Containing Seven Books of the Jewish War and Two Books against Apion. William Whiston, M.A. Sometime Professor of Mathematics in the University of Cambridge, London 1737. https://penelope.uchicago.edu/josephus/war-6.html
[9] History of the Christian Church & Ecclesiastical History by Paul Schaff ISBN 978-80-268-9775-0, II:8

Matthew 24:8 (NASB)—Birth Pangs

But all these things are merely the beginning of birth pangs.

It is common today for people trained in the futurist view to look at present-day natural disasters and claim that they are signs of the imminent return of Jesus, yet that is not what Jesus said.

He was very clear that these signs would happen within that generation; furthermore, they would not be signs of the end of the world but "merely the beginning of birth pangs."

These birth pangs were to precede the destruction of Jerusalem and the Temple.

John Chrysostom (349-407) Archbishop of Constantinople was an important Early Church Father.

He speaks of the preludes to the troubles of the Jews. "All this is but the beginning of the birth pangs," that is, of the troubles that will befall them. (The Ancient Christian Commentary, 2002, Ib: 190)

Matthew 24:9: Persecution/Tribulation

Then they will deliver you to tribulation, and will kill you, and you will be hated by all nations because of My name.

The Jewish religious leaders instigated the first persecution. Saul was among those leaders who oversaw the men who were putting Christians to death. The Book of Acts describes that persecution, saying in Acts 8:1

Now Saul was consenting to his death. At that time a great persecution arose against the church which was at Jerusalem; and they were all scattered throughout the regions of Judea and Samaria, except the Apostles.

That "great persecution" continued to spread, and soon government officials such as King Herod got involved: as revealed in Acts 12:1-3

Now about that time Herod the king stretched out his hand to harass some from the church. Then he killed James the brother of John with the sword. And because he saw that it pleased the Jews, he proceeded further to seize Peter also.

The persecution became even more intense in A.D. 64. That was the year when more than one third of the city of Rome burned to the ground. The significance of that event is difficult for us to grasp, on several levels.

For example, if we compared it with the destruction of the Twin Towers in New York City, we would have to say that the fire in Rome was several times more devastating. At that time Rome was considered the center of the civilized world, and more than one third of the city was destroyed.

Nero, who was the emperor at that time, blamed Christians for that terrible fire, and then he began what Church historians call "The Great Persecution."

The historian, Tacitus (c. A.D. 55-120), wrote how thousands of Christians were tortured, being covered in animal skins then torn to death by dogs, or being nailed to crosses, or being covered in tar and then lit on fire to illuminate Nero's gardens while he entertained guests in the evenings.

Matthew 24:10-13: Apostasy and False Prophets

And then many will be offended, will betray one another, and will hate one another. Then many false prophets will rise up and deceive many. And because lawlessness will abound, the love of many will grow cold. But he who endures to the end shall be saved.

Soon after the death of our Lord, false prophets began appearing on the scene.

Apostle Paul warned his followers to watch out for the false prophets. We see this example in Acts 20:17-32 before Paul departed to Rome for the final time.

And from Miletus he sent to Ephesus, and called the elders of the church. And when they were come to him, he said unto them, Ye know, from the first day that I came into Asia, after what manner I have been with you at all seasons, Serving the LORD with all humility of mind, and with many tears, and temptations, which befell me by the lying in wait of the Jews: And how I kept back nothing that was profitable unto you, but have shewed you, and have taught you publicly, and from house to house, Testifying both to the Jews, and also to the Greeks, repentance toward God, and faith toward our

Lord Jesus Christ. And now, behold, I go bound in the spirit unto Jerusalem, not knowing the things that shall befall me there: Save that the Holy Ghost witnesseth in every city, saying that bonds and afflictions abide me. But none of these things move me, neither count I my life dear unto myself, so that I might finish my course with joy, and the ministry, which I have received of the Lord Jesus, to testify the gospel of the grace of God. And now, behold, I know that ye all, among whom I have gone preaching the kingdom of God, shall see my face no more. Wherefore I take you to record this day, that I am pure from the blood of all men. For I have not shunned to declare unto you all the counsel of God. Take heed therefore unto yourselves, and to all the flock, over the which the Holy Ghost hath made you overseers, to feed the church of God, which he hath purchased with his own blood. For I know this, that after my departing shall grievous wolves enter in among you, not sparing the flock. Also of your own selves shall men arise, speaking perverse things, to draw away disciples after them. Therefore watch, and remember, that by the space of three years I ceased not to warn every one night and day with tears. And now, brethren, I commend you to God, and to the word of his grace, which is able to build you up, and to give you an inheritance among all them which are sanctified.

Apostle John stated implicitly that during his lifetime "many false prophets have gone out into the world" 1 John 4:1-3.

Beloved, believe not every spirit, but try the spirits whether they are of God: because many false prophets are gone out into the world. Hereby know ye the Spirit of God: Every spirit that confesseth that Jesus Christ is come in the flesh is of God: And every spirit that confesseth not that Jesus Christ is come in the flesh is not of God: and this is that spirit of antichrist, whereof ye have heard that it should come; and even now already is it in the world. KJV

Similarly, Apostle Peter warned, in 2 Peter 2:1-5, False prophets also arose among the people, just as there will also be false teachers among you, who will secretly introduce destructive heresies. You can read the entire Chapter!

But there were false prophets also among the people, even as there shall be false teachers among you, who privily shall bring in damnable heresies, even denying the Lord that bought them, and bring upon themselves swift destruction. And many shall follow their pernicious ways; by reason of whom the way of truth shall be evil spoken of. And through covetousness shall they with feigned words make merchandise of you: whose judgment now of a long time lingereth not, and their damnation slumbereth not. For if God spared not the angels that sinned, but cast them down to hell, and delivered them into chains of darkness, to be reserved unto judgment; And spared not the old world, but saved Noah the eighth person, a preacher of righteousness, bringing in the flood upon the world of the ungodly; KJV

The first major group was the Judaizers, who taught that Gentiles had to become Jewish proselytes and adhere to the Law of Moses as well as have faith in Christ.

Then came the Gnostics. They arose as soon as Christians brought the gospel to Greek-minded people, but by the year A.D. 150, about one third of all Christians were involved in Gnosticism.

To grasp the influence of this heresy, imagine how it would be today if one third of all Christians in your own community were taken in by a certain heretical teaching. That is exactly what happened during those early days when the Church was struggling to survive.

A Brief Understanding of Gnosticism

The name is derived from the Greek word *"gnosis"* which literally means *"knowledge."*

- At the foundation of First-Century Gnosticism was a worldview in which the spiritual world was distinctly separated from the natural world.
- The spiritual world was considered good, and the natural world was considered corrupt.
- The leaders of this teaching/belief concluded that God could not have taken on flesh or come into this corrupt world in the form of Jesus. This led to several false teachings about the nature of Jesus.

- Thinking of this natural world as corrupt also led them to believe that a person must be very spirit-conscious to be a good Christian. Hence, they developed mystical understandings and taught that a person must have secret knowledge to know God. From this the word Gnosticism came, for it literally means "knowledge."
- During the First Century, Gnosticism took many forms, but one of the most influential Gnostic groups completely rejected the Old Testament. They declared that the God of the Old Testament was the devil and Jesus had come to reveal an "unknown Father" to us.
- Other Gnostics taught that the Old Testament rituals were still valid for Christians.
- One of the most prominent Gnostic teachers was a man called Cerinthus. He was a Jew who lived in Asia Minor, teaching that Jesus was the son of Joseph and Mary (not born of a virgin)—an ordinary man. A heavenly spirit called "the Christ" came upon Jesus at His baptism and left Him at the crucifixion. Jesus had brought secret teachings that would enable people to overcome enslavement to the physical world, but the Jewish customs also had to be observed. Those who proved faithful to these teachings and observances would live for a literal 1,000 years of sensual pleasures. These teachings of Cerinthus flourished throughout Asia Minor.
- Historical records tell us that the Apostle John was so horrified at Cerinthus' teachings that on one occasion when John walked into the public baths with his disciples at Ephesus, he saw Cerinthus and ran out of the bathhouse, warning his disciples that the house may fall down because "Cerinthus, the enemy of the truth, is inside."
- This is the setting in which Apostle John ministered. History tells us that by the year A.D. 150, one third of all Christians were under the influence of Gnosticism. It was a huge cult and a major concern of the Church fathers. John was on the front lines of that battle.

<u>Apostle John wrote to correct Gnostic Teachings as soon as we learn about the historical setting in which he ministered, we can more easily understand his writings.</u>

- For example, his Gospel starts off saying: In the beginning was the Word, and the Word was with God, and the Word was God... And the Word became flesh, and dwelt among us, and we saw His glory. (John 1:1-14)

- Do you see how profound this statement is? Because the Gnostics thought of the natural world as evil, they could not believe that Jesus could have been God and at the same time have taken on human flesh. John boldly told the reader that he saw Jesus. Jesus was real. Jesus came into this world. John declared that Jesus is God and Jesus took on flesh.
- John was also countering Gnosticism when he wrote his first Two Epistles. First John starts with a declaration that is diametrically opposed to the Gnostic view of Jesus. 1 John 1:1-2

What was from the beginning, what we have heard, what we have seen with our eyes, what we have looked at and touched with our hands, concerning the Word of Life—and the life was manifested, and we have seen and testify and proclaim to you the eternal life, which was with the Father and was manifested to us.

Do you see how clearly and forcefully John is confronting Gnosticism here? John said that he and the other Apostles heard Jesus, saw Him, and touched Him with their hands. Jesus manifested Himself in this world. He was God, and He took on flesh. This battle that John had with Gnosticism is common knowledge among Bible scholars. In fact, any student serious about understanding John's writings will be ever conscious of this fact.

Matthew 24:14: Preaching the Gospel

What about Matthew 24:14?

This gospel of the kingdom shall be preached in the whole world as a testimony to all the nations, and then the end will come.

If you have been trained under the futurist view, you know that this verse is often quoted to encourage Christians to help get the Gospel spread around the world so that Jesus Christ can return. And YES, we must preach the Gospel of The Kingdom, UNTIL Jesus Returns...

However: Let Us Look at Another Way to Understand This Scripture.

Jesus said that all of the events of which He spoke would happen in that generation. If we are going to believe the Words of Jesus literally, then we must look to see how this verse could have been fulfilled in the First Century.

For example, for us to understand Matthew 24:14, it will be helpful to find out if there are other Bible passages that talk about the gospel being preached to the whole world. If you do this in your own study, you will discover five passages that address this subject. Amazingly, all five passages reveal to us how the Gospel was proclaimed to all nations within the generation of the Apostles. Let's look at those five passages.

First, examine the words of Apostle Paul in Romans 1:8:

First, I thank my God through Jesus Christ for you all, because your faith is being proclaimed throughout the whole world.

Their faith is being proclaimed—in Paul's lifetime—throughout the whole world.

Apostle Paul makes this even clearer in Romans 10:18:

But I say, surely they have never heard, have they? Indeed they have; Their voice has gone out into all the earth, and their words to the ends of the world.

Apostle Paul says this again in Romans 16:25-26:

Now to Him who is able to establish you according to my gospel and the preaching of Jesus Christ, according to the revelation of the mystery which has been kept secret for long ages past, but now is manifested, and by the Scriptures of the prophets, according to the commandment of the eternal God, has been made known to all the nations, leading to obedience of faith;

According to my (Apostle Paul's message) gospel and the preaching of Jesus Christ . . . has been made known to all the nations (in Apostle Paul's time, over 2000 years ago).

Apostle Paul tells us this again in Colossians 1:5-6:

because of the hope laid up for you in heaven, of which you previously heard in the word of truth, the gospel which has come to you, just as in all the world also it is constantly bearing fruit and increasing, even as it has been doing in you also since the day you heard of it and understood the grace of God in truth;

The gospel which has come to you, just as in all the world also it is constantly bearing fruit and increasing.

There it is again. The gospel was bearing fruit in all the world—in Paul's lifetime.

Finally, Let's Look at The Clearest Statement Paul Made on This Subject: Colossians 1:23

If indeed you continue in the faith firmly established and steadfast, and not moved away from the hope of the gospel that you have heard, which was proclaimed in all creation under heaven, and of which I, Paul, was made a minister.

Could Paul have stated it any clearer? The gospel was proclaimed "in all creation under heaven."

As folks read these passages they may wonder if the words "whole world," "ends of the world," "all the world," and "all creation under heaven," really mean the whole world in the way we understand today. Some may question if these words perhaps meant the world as far as the Disciples knew it or just the Roman Empire.

In these passages there are two different Greek words that have been translated into the word "world." Paul used the Greek word kosmos in Romans 1:8 and in Colossians 1:6.

The word kosmos can be translated as "world" or "earth," but either way, it includes the entire world.

The other Greek word for world is oikoumene, which can be translated "inhabited earth" or "civilized earth." Paul used this word in Romans 10:18, when he declared that the Word had gone out "to the ends of the world."

Jesus also used this word, oikoumene, in Matthew 24:14.

Hence, we understand that His original declaration was that the Disciples would have time to preach the gospel of the Kingdom to the then civilized world.

However, we look at it, the Words of Jesus were fulfilled within the generation of the First Disciples. They did turn the world upside down.

After they preached the gospel successfully, Jesus said, "*and then the end will come*" (Matthew 24:14).

What End Was He Referring To?

Remember, He was answering their question, "When will Jerusalem and the Temple be destroyed?" That is the "END" about which Jesus was speaking. Indeed, that destruction is what Jesus talked about next.

The Temple of God—His Dwelling Place

Please remember this: God's first interaction with mankind began in the Garden where He would come and have Fellowship with Adam and Eve in the cool of the day.

After they sinned and God rose up a People to Himself (the Jews), He instructed Moses to pitch a Tent in which He would come and interact with them...

King Solomon built the first permanent Temple in 957 BC on direct orders from God. And it replaced the Tent... The dimensions were very specific, and we all know what occurred when the first Temple was dedicated... God's Glory came down and filled it.

During the ensuing years many attempts were made by the heathen nations to destroy It; but they were all unsuccessful until 586 BC when It was completely destroyed by the Babylonians when they sacked the city...

According to the Book of Ezra, work on building (rebuilding) the Second Temple began in 538 BC, which was authorized by King Cyrus, the Great under the direct orders from God. God called King Cyrus; His Anointed! It was completed 23 years later and was dedicated in 515 BC.

Several attempts were made to destroy it after being rebuilt and dedicated in 515 BC but they were all unsuccessful.

And it was not until AD 70 that the Temple was completely destroyed, fulfilling the Prophecy of Jesus the Messiah; that Not One Stone was going to be left on top one another.

There was never any mandate given by God for it to be rebuilt. As a matter of fact, Jesus Christ had already begun to declare that His Father's true intent was never for Him to dwell in Temples made with hands of men or by mortal men. Or that He never intended for that Worship to Him would be done from a "Specific, Physical Holy Place" as was revealed through His conversation with the Woman at The Well:

John 4:19-26

The woman said to Him, "Sir, I perceive that You are a prophet. Our fathers worshiped on this mountain, and you Jews say that in Jerusalem is the place where one ought to worship." Jesus said to her, "Woman, believe Me, the hour is coming when you will neither on this mountain, nor in Jerusalem, worship the Father. You worship what you do not know; we know what we worship, for salvation is of the Jews. But the hour is coming, and now is, when the true worshipers will worship the Father in spirit and truth; for the Father is seeking such to worship Him. God is Spirit, and those who worship Him must worship in spirit and truth." The woman said to Him, "I know that Messiah is coming" (who is called Christ). "When He comes, He will tell us all things." Jesus said to her, "I who speak to you am He."

Acts 7:44-50

Our fathers had the tabernacle of witness in the wilderness, as He appointed, instructing Moses to make it according to the pattern that he had seen, which our fathers, having received it in turn, also brought with Joshua into the land possessed by the Gentiles, whom God drove out before the face of our fathers until the days of David, who found favour before God and asked to find a dwelling for the God of Jacob. But Solomon built Him a house. "However, the Most High does not dwell in temples made with hands, as the prophet says: 'Heaven is My throne, And earth is My footstool. What house will you build for Me? says the LORD, Or what is the place of My rest? Has My hand not made all these things?'

Acts 17:16-25

Now while Paul waited for them at Athens, his spirit was provoked within him when he saw that the city was given over to idols. Therefore he reasoned in the synagogue with the Jews and with the Gentile worshipers, and in the marketplace daily with those who happened to be there. Then certain Epicurean and Stoic philosophers encountered him. And some said, "What does this babbler want to say?" Others said, "He seems to be a proclaimer of foreign gods," because he preached to them Jesus and the resurrection. And they took him and brought him to the Areopagus, saying, "May we know what this new doctrine is of which you speak? For you are bringing some strange things to our ears. Therefore we want to know what these things mean." For all the Athenians and the foreigners who were there spent their time in nothing else but either to tell or to hear some new thing. Then Paul stood in the midst of the Areopagus and said, "Men of Athens, I perceive that in all things you are very religious; for as I was passing through and considering the objects of your worship, I even found an altar with this inscription: TO THE UNKNOWN GOD. Therefore, the One whom you worship without knowing, Him I proclaim to you: God, who made the world and everything in it, since He is Lord of heaven and earth, does not dwell in temples made with hands. Nor is He worshiped with men's hands, as though He needed anything, since He gives to all life, breath, and all things."

So, no matter what popular opinion says—God did not and has not authorized any rebuilding of the Jewish temple. And if for any reason one is rebuilt God will NOT be taking up residence there...

Matthew 24:15-20: Warning of Destruction

Jesus told the Disciples that after they successfully preached the gospel in every nation or in the then inhabited earth; they needed to be ready to flee from Judea, because destruction was about to occur.

Therefore when you see the abomination of desolation, which was spoken of through Daniel the prophet, standing in the holy place (let the reader understand), then those who are in Judea must flee to the mountains. Whoever is on the housetop must not go down to get the things out that are in his house. Whoever is in the field must not turn back to get his cloak. But woe to those who are pregnant and to those who are nursing babies in those days! But pray that your flight will not be in the winter, or on a Sabbath.

Christians trained in the futurist view envision this passage being fulfilled in the future before the end of the world. Typically, they think of the abomination of desolation as the antichrist who will walk into the Temple (one that they declare, will be built in the near future) in Jerusalem, set up an idol of himself, and declare himself as God. That event is thought to begin a terrible worldwide tribulation.

To understand this passage; please note that Jesus is talking about tragic events that will happen not throughout the world, but right there in Jerusalem and the surrounding area of Judea.

We know this because He is talking to His Disciples and answering their question about when Jerusalem and the Temple will be destroyed.

Jesus said that when the abomination of desolation (which we will define later) stands in the Holy Place, people "in Judea" are to run to the mountains.

He Did Not Say That People All Over the World Should Flee.

Further, we know that Jesus was addressing His warning to the Jews, for He warned people to pray that their flight may not be on the Sabbath—a warning that is particularly relevant to Jewish people, as they kept the Sabbath in a fashion that did not allow them to work or run—even in the event of a tragedy.

Also, He said that people on their housetops must not go into their houses to get their possessions; that, too, indicates that He was talking about people in that region of the world, for houses in Jerusalem often were constructed in a way in which people could gather on their rooftops.

Jesus' warning tells us nothing about people living outside of Judea.

Jesus was speaking of something terrible about to happen in Judea, and there is nothing in the passage to indicate a worldwide event.

The Parallel Passages Are in Mark 13 and Luke 21

To confirm that Jesus was speaking in Matthew 24:15-20 of events to happen around Jerusalem and Judea, it is helpful to glance at the Gospels of Mark and Luke where the Olivet Discourse is also recorded.

In looking at these parallel passages, it is worth noting how closely they correspond with Matthew 24.

Jesus exposed the wickedness of the Jewish religious leaders and pronounced condemnation and judgement upon them... (Matthew 23:1-35; Mark 12:38-40; Luke 20:45-47).

Jesus declared the Temple's destruction (Matthew 23:37-24:2; Mark 13:1-2 Luke 21:5-6 The Disciples questioned Jesus about the coming destruction (Matthew 24:3; Mark 13:3-4; Luke 21:7).

Jesus answered, talking about:

- •People claiming to be Christ (Matthew 24:5; Mark 13:5-6; Luke 21:8)!
- •Wars and rumours of war (Matthew 24:6-7; Mark 13:7-8; Luke 21:9-10)!
- • Earthquakes and famines (Matthew 24:7; Mark 13:8; Luke 21:11)!
- • And the gospel being preached all over the then world (Matthew 24:14; Mark 13:10)!

These passages are amazingly similar, although each writer used slightly different terminology. After Jesus talked about the signs that would take place, He went on in each Gospel to warn that people would have to flee from Judea.

Let's Examine the Accounts in The Three Parallel Passages.

Therefore when you see the abomination of desolation which was spoken of through Daniel the prophet, standing in the holy place (let the reader understand), then those who are in Judea must flee to the mountains. (Matthew 24:15-16)

But when you see Jerusalem surrounded by armies, then recognize that her desolation is near. Then those who are in Judea must flee to the mountains. (Luke 21:20-21)

But when you see the abomination of desolation standing where it should not be (let the reader understand), then those who are in Judea must flee to the mountains. (Mark 13:14)

Notice that in all three passages Jesus clearly states that it is the people in Judea who are to flee! Nowhere in any of the passages does He speak of or refer to any broader region.

Let us now explore what the Scriptures teach concerning an abomination of desolation standing in the holy place. Again, this may surprise you. For many believe that this has to do with something in the Twenty-First Century.

The Abomination of Desolation:

Now we need to examine what Jesus was referring to when He warned the Disciples about an abomination of desolation standing in the holy place.

As mentioned earlier, futurist teachers assume that the abomination is the antichrist who will setup an idol in a future temple or actually step into that temple and declare himself as God.

To see how unfounded that understanding is, first note that the antichrist is never mentioned in Matthew 24 (nor in any of the Gospels).

Also, note that Jesus was talking to His Disciples and telling them that they will witness this event.

Jesus was not talking about an antichrist who would come hundreds or even thousands of years later, but rather some abomination that would be seen in their lifetime.

The Holy Place

Next, we can identify where the abomination was to stand. Matthew refers to the "Holy Place" and Luke refers to "Jerusalem." Which author is correct? Both.

When Matthew mentions the Holy Place, he was referring to the same location as Luke when he referred to Jerusalem.

We can confirm this by examining the terminology "holy place," which has been translated from the Greek words hagios topos. This terminology is never used anywhere in the Bible to refer to the Temple or the holy of holies in the Temple (where futurist teachers declare the anti-Christ will sit).

As anyone with a Greek dictionary can learn, the word hagios means holy and the word topos refers to a locality. It is used in expressions such as a "desert place" but never in reference to a building.

Since we have Luke referring to this holy place as "Jerusalem," it is logical to assume that Jesus was referring to Jerusalem in the parallel passage of Matthew.

Next, What Is the Abomination of Desolation? When we speak of an abomination, we are referring to a horrible, detestable, disgusting thing.

Luke tells us that the abomination was the armies surrounding Jerusalem. What could be more detestable to Jewish people?

But when you see Jerusalem surrounded by armies, then recognize that her desolation is near. Then those who are in Judea must flee to the mountains. (Luke 21:20-21)

The Heathen Armies Would Gather to Make the Holy City A Desolation.

Does This Correspond with Historical Evidence? Perfectly!

As we have noted, in the year A.D.70, twenty thousand Roman soldiers lined the mountains around Jerusalem, surrounding the holy city.

John Chrysostom (349-407)) writes, "the abomination of desolation means the army by which the holy city of Jerusalem was made desolate." (The Ante-Nicene Fathers)

This description also matches the one we read in Daniel Chapter 9. Remember that Jesus referred in Matthew 24:15 to the abomination of desolation "about which Daniel spoke." Note Daniel's reference to the abomination:

The people of the prince who is to come will destroy the city and the sanctuary. And its end will come with a flood; even to the end there will be war; desolations are determined. (Daniel 9:26)

Indeed, the soldiers came to destroy Jerusalem. For four months they starved the people; and then they proceeded to descend upon the city as a flood pouring into the valley. Fleeing Jerusalem and Judea When the abomination—that is, the Roman soldiers—began lining the mountains around Jerusalem, there was a short time during which people could flee. Hence, we can understand our Lord's exhortation for those on the housetops not to go down to get their possessions, nor those in the field to return to get their cloaks. Jesus was telling them that they must flee immediately.

After those Christians in Jerusalem were allowed to escape, the Roman soldiers sealed off the city. No one else was allowed to go in or out. The Romans cut Jerusalem off so the people would starve.

Josephus wrote: So, all hope of escaping was now cut off from the Jews, together with their liberty of going out of the city. Then did the famine widen its progress and devoured the people by whole houses and families; the upper rooms were full of women and children that were dying by famine; and the lanes of the city were full of the dead bodies of the aged; the children also and the young men wandered about the marketplaces like shadows, all swelled with the famine, and fell down dead, wheresoever their misery seized them. (The Wars of the Jews, 1998, v:xii:3)

Historically, we know that the early Disciples fled Jerusalem before the destruction of the city. Why did they flee? Because they remembered the warning that Jesus gave them that armies would surround the city and as such, they must flee to escape the devastation that would follow.

Eusebius: The members of the Jerusalem church, by means of an oracle given by revelation to acceptable persons there, were ordered to leave the City before the war began and settle in a town in Peraea called Pella. (The History of the Church, 1965, III:5)

The Venerable Bede: When on the approach of the war with Rome and the extermination of the Jewish people, all the Christians who were in that province, warned by the prophecy, fled far away, as Church history relates, and retiring beyond Jordan, remained for a time in the city of Pella. (Cited in Thomas Aquinas' Golden Chain, Dec. 1, 07,)

Charles Spurgeon: The Christians in Jerusalem and the surrounding towns and villages, "in Judea", availed themselves of the first opportunity for eluding the Roman armies, and fled to the mountain city of Pella, where they were preserved from the general destruction which overthrew the Jews. There was no time to spare before the final investment of the guilty city; the man "on the house-top" could "not come down to take anything out of his house", and the man "in the field" could not "return back, to take his clothes." They must flee to the mountains in the greatest haste the moment that they saw "Jerusalem compassed with armies." (The Gospel of the Kingdom, 1974, p. 215)

John Chrysostom: "Then let those who are in Judea flee to the mountains." When does he mean by "then"? When these things will take place, he says, "When you see the desolating sacrilege spoken of by the Prophet Daniel, standing in the holy place." He seems to me to be speaking of the armies and wars. So, flee. There is no hope of safety for you in the cities. (The Ancient Christian Commentary, 2002, Ib: 193)

Matthew 24:21-22: A Great Tribulation

Jesus warned the Disciples to flee from Judea (Matthew 24:15-20). Then He prophesied the great destruction to follow: Matthew 24:21-22

For then there will be a great tribulation, such as has not occurred since the beginning of the world until now, nor ever will. Unless those days had been cut short, no life would have been saved; but for the sake of the elect those days will be cut short.

Futurist teachers say that this great tribulation will come in the future, just before the end of the world, and it will spread over all the earth. This coming tribulation is talked about so much in some Christian circles that it has developed its own identity and is called "The Great Tribulation." In reality, Jesus was talking about the destruction of Jerusalem in A.D. 70. He was answering the Disciples' question, "When will Jerusalem and the Temple be destroyed?

If Jesus truly was talking about the events of A.D. 70, then we have another question to answer. How could He have said that nothing so terrible has occurred since the beginning of the world until now, nor ever will?

Haven't there been more wicked things happen than the destruction of Jerusalem?

What about the Twentieth-Century Holocaust when six million Jews were murdered?

What about other times of war and mass destruction?

The destruction of Jerusalem was not the greatest in magnitude, but Jesus was talking in terms of it being the greatest calamity in the sense of suffering and anguish.

Josephus Describes for Us What Actually Took Place in A.D. 70.

After the Roman soldiers sealed off the city, Josephus tells how the Jews committed terrible atrocities to each other, even horrific actions, such as cannibalism, which occurred during the famine. He narrates a vile account of a woman murdering her small son, cooking him, and eating half of him, then arguing with thieves, who broke into her house looking for food, as to who would eat the other half. During the famine, Jews also swallowed diamonds and precious stones in hopes of escaping and safely carrying them to new locations. Knowing this, the Roman soldiers would capture individuals from the city and cut open their stomachs and entrails, searching for whatever they could find. After General Titus put an end to those searches, a new form of torture began. Josephus wrote that as men tried to escape the city or to crawl out to gather food, the Roman soldiers would cut off their hands and send them back inside the city. When the Roman soldiers finally were given the order to descend upon Jerusalem, Josephus tells us that more than 500 men were caught per day, then whipped, tortured, and crucified. Men were nailed to crosses in front of the city until there was no more space. Finally, the soldiers entered the city, and every person was killed except for 97,000, who were taken away to be slaves in the Egyptian mines or as gifts to various provinces so that they might be killed in the theatres. When Jerusalem was destroyed, a genocide of Jews was triggered throughout the surrounding regions. Josephus said: There was not any one Syrian city, which did not slay their Jewish inhabitants, and were not more bitter enemies to us than were the Romans themselves. (The Wars of the Jews, 1998, vii:viii)

History provides many similar reports of what took place throughout the whole of the Roman Empire. When we compare the genocide of A.D. 70 to the Jewish Holocaust of the Twentieth Century, we must admit that the more recent Holocaust was greater in number, with 6 million Jews killed over a six-year period. Living in labour camps and being killed with poisonous gas was horrific, but as far as we know, no one was crucified. In A.D. 70 more than one million Jews were starved, tortured and killed in a four-month period. Despite the Twentieth Century Holocaust's larger magnitude, the violence during the A.D. 70 tribulation ended the lives of a much greater percentage of the Jewish population and was far more extreme in the atrocities that were committed.

Charles Spurgeon: The destruction of Jerusalem was more terrible than anything that the world has ever witnessed, either before or since. Even Titus seemed to see in his cruel work the hand of an avenging God. Truly, the blood of the martyrs slain in Jerusalem was amply avenged when the whole city became a veritable Aceldama, or field of blood. (Spurgeon's Popular Exposition of Matthew, 1979, p. 211)

Eusebius: Thousands and thousands of men of every age who together with women and children perished by the sword, by starvation, and by countless other forms of death... all this anyone who wishes can gather in precise detail from the pages of Josephus's history. I must draw particular attention to his statement that the people who flocked together from all Judaea at the time of the Passover Feast and—to use his own words— were shut up in Jerusalem as if in a prison, totalled nearly three million. (The History of the Church, 1965, p. 69)

Matthew 24:23-27: False Christs Appear

As people were being slaughtered throughout Judea, many Jews held to their hopes of a Messiah appearing to deliver them at the last moment.

Several leaders took advantage of this belief, which was so fundamental to the Jewish heart and mind.

Knowing that this would happen, Jesus gave a warning:

"Then if anyone says to you, 'Behold, here is the Christ,' or 'There He is,' do not believe him. For false Christs and false prophets will arise and will show great signs and wonders, so as to mislead, if possible, even the elect. Behold, I have told you in advance. So if they say to you, 'Behold, He is in the wilderness,' do not go out, or 'Behold, He is in the inner rooms,' do not believe them. For just as the lightning comes from the east and flashes even to the west, so will the coming of the Son of Man be." (Matthew 24:23-27)

Josephus Wrote of Many False Prophets and Leaders Claiming to Be the Christ.

One example he gave was of a false prophet who publicly declared to the desperate Jerusalem dwellers, that on a certain day, God was going to supernaturally deliver them. Many Jews followed that leader and ended up losing their lives because of their false hope. Josephus also described how extraordinary signs appeared, including a star resembling a sword over Jerusalem and then a light around the Temple for a half hour. (The War of The Jews)

Just As Jesus Had Prophesied, The False Christs Demonstrated "Great Signs and Wonders."

Saint Jerome: (347-420) At the time of the Jewish captivity by Rome, many Jewish elders claimed to be the Christ. There were so many, in fact, that there were three distinct camps of them when the Romans besieged Jerusalem. (The Ancient Christian Commentary, 2002, Ib: 197)

Jesus warned the Disciples not to listen to any rumours or declarations of Christ or false prophets appearing. Then He made a declaration contrasting the false to the real. He said: "For just as the lightning comes from the east and flashes even to the west, so will the coming of the Son of Man be." (Matthew 24:23-27) From this they were to know that Jesus' coming would not happen in the wilderness or in some secret place. When the Messiah truly came, Jesus said, it would happen up above.

Matthew 24:28: The Corpse and Vultures

Wherever the corpse is, there the vultures will gather.

Envision thousands of soldiers gathered on the mountains encircling Jerusalem. Now add to that picture the banner under which they assembled—the banner of the vulture, which Roman soldiers carried on flags and often painted on their shields. As a Prophet, Jesus declared that the vultures would gather, and Jerusalem would be the corpse.

Confirmation From the Parallel Gospels

Jesus finished answering the first question, having explained all of the signs that would lead up to the destruction of Jerusalem and the Temple.

Before we go on to examine His answer to the second question, it is worth pointing out the confirmation of two other Gospels. We discussed how closely Mark 13 and Luke 21 parallel Matthew 24. There is, however, one key difference. In Matthew 24:3 the disciples asked Jesus three questions:

Question #1: "When will these things happen?"
Question #2: "What will be the sign of Your coming?"
Question #3: "What about the end of the age (world)?"

In contrast, neither Mark nor Luke records the second or third questions. Luke 21:5-7 goes like this:

And while some were talking about the temple, that it was adorned with beautiful stones and votive gifts, He said, "As for these things which you are looking at, the days will come in which there will not be left one stone upon another which will not be torn down." They questioned Him, saying, "Teacher, when therefore will these things happen? And what will be the sign when these things are about to take place?" NASB

Mark 13:1-4 reads very similarly to this passage, without asking anything about the signs of our Lord's coming or of the end of the world.

*As He was going out of the temple, one of His disciples *said to Him, "Teacher, behold what wonderful stones and what wonderful*

buildings!" And Jesus said to him, "Do you see these great build-ings? Not one stone will be left upon another which will not be torn down." As He was sitting on the Mount of Olives opposite the temple, Peter and James and John and Andrew were questioning Him privately, "Tell us, when will these things be, and what will be the sign when all these things are going to be fulfilled?" NASB

This is significant because it gives us a clear framework in which to understand Matthew Chapter 24. Since Mark and Luke record only the question about when the Temple would be destroyed, we know that our Lord was answering that question when He talked about people claiming to be Christ, wars, earthquakes, famines, persecutions, etc.

The answers Jesus gave in Mark and Luke are almost identical to the answers He gave in Matthew 24:4-22. Therefore, it is only reasonable to conclude that Jesus was talking about the Temple's destruction when He talked about people claiming to be Christ, wars, earthquakes, famines, persecutions, etc. This Is Confirmation That Matthew 24:4-22 Is Answering the First Question Only.

Acknowledging the parallels in the Gospels shows again how wrong futurist teachers are when they try to combine all three questions recorded in Matthew 24:3, as if they all are asking about the "Second Coming" and the end of the world.

We will look at the answers Jesus gave to the two remaining questions, and, indeed, we will talk about His coming and the end of the world, because those are the second and third questions. However, make no mistake that the first question was about the destruction of Jerusalem and the Temple. That happened in A.D. 70, within the generation of the disciples, exactly as Jesus prophesied.

Closing The First Question – A Few Points to Note:

We cannot emphasize enough how significant an event it was when Jerusalem and the Temple were destroyed.

Jerusalem was the "Holy City."

•Mount Moriah, upon which the Temple stood, was the site where Abraham was willing to offer his son Isaac (Genesis 22:2).
• It was also the place where God appeared to David (2 Chronicles 3:1).

- It was the site upon which Solomon had built the first Temple. It was there that the High Priests offered sacrifices for the sins of the people.
- It was the centre of Jewish life, a deeply sacred site.
- When the Temple was destroyed, the Jewish heritage was destroyed. In one sense, they were cut off from God. They lost their identity. Their religious system was abolished.

Remember that the writer of Hebrews explained how the Jewish religious system was abolished and replaced with the New Covenant established through Jesus when He said:

A new covenant, He has made the first obsolete. But whatever is becoming obsolete and growing old is ready to disappear. (Hebrews 8:13) NASB

We have a New Covenant with better promises.

We have a High Priest (Jesus Christ) who has made the ultimate and final sacrifice.

- The transition from the Old to the New stands at the centre of history and the Bible.
- It is a pivotal point in God's plan through the ages.

When the Temple in Jerusalem was destroyed, it finalized the end of the old religious system.

So, this brings an end to the study of the first question the disciples posed to Jesus and the answer He gave them. Now let us explore their second question and the answer that Jesus gave them!

Question #2: "What Will Be the Sign of Your Coming?"

We have already explained how all of the signs, such as wars, earthquakes, famines, etc., were signs preceding the destruction of the Temple in A.D. 70. Those signs were fulfilled. They are not for our future, although we have had them and will continue to have them.

Now we need to determine what the Disciples meant when they asked, "What will be the sign of Your coming?"

When people read that question today, they have a very different mind-set than the disciples had 2,000 years ago.

When the Disciples were sitting with Jesus on the Mount of Olives, they were not thinking about the Second Coming of our Lord. In fact, at that time in their lives they were not convinced that Jesus was going to die, let alone return to earth someday, as clearly shown in the following Scripture:

Matthew 16:21-23

From that time Jesus began to show to His disciples that He must go to Jerusalem, and suffer many things from the elders and chief priests and scribes, and be killed, and be raised the third day. Then Peter took Him aside and began to rebuke Him, saying, "Far be it from You, Lord; this shall not happen to You!" But He turned and said to Peter, "Get behind Me, Satan! You are an offense to Me, for you are not mindful of the things of God, but the things of men."

Therefore, they could not have been asking about the "Second Coming". What, then, were they asking? Look again at the question:

"What will be the sign of Your coming?"

What does His "coming" mean? —at that time in history, the Jews were looking for a Messiah. That was their primary hope. They were looking for a Messiah to come and set up a kingdom in which the Jews would have dominion over the whole earth and reign forever.

Knowing this, gives us an entirely different outlook on the thinking of the disciples. Remember when the mother of the sons of Zebedee asked Jesus if her two sons could sit, one on His right and the other on His left (Matthew 20:20-23)?

Then the mother of Zebedee's sons came to Him with her sons, kneeling down and asking something from Him. And He said to her, "What do you wish?" She said to Him, "Grant that these two sons of mine may sit, one on Your right hand and the other on the left, in Your kingdom." But Jesus answered and said, "You do not know what you ask. Are you able to drink the cup that I am about to drink, and be baptized with the baptism that I am baptized with?" They said to Him, "We are able." So He said to them, "You will indeed drink My cup, and be baptized with the baptism that I am baptized with; but to sit on My right hand and on My left is not Mine to give, but it is for those for whom it is prepared by My Father."

That reveals what was on their minds. When the disciples asked Jesus, "What will be the sign of Your coming?" they were asking Him, "When will You come into Your kingdom?" "When will You take Your position and reveal Yourself as king?"

When did that happen?

After Jesus died, rose from the dead, and ascended into heaven, He sat down on the throne at the right hand of God the Father.

All authority was given to Him, both in heaven and earth.

Jesus came into His Kingdom the moment He ascended into heaven and sat down next to the Father. It happened almost 2,000 years ago, in the generation in which the disciples lived.

To confirm this, read the words of Jesus in Matthew 16:28:

"Truly I say to you, there are some of those who are standing here who will not taste death until they see the Son of Man coming in His kingdom." NASB

Similarly, Mark records the words of Jesus:

"There are some of those who are standing here who will not taste death until they see the kingdom of God after it has come with power." (Mark 9:1) NASB

Could Jesus have said it any clearer? He declared that some of the people who were alive at that time in history would live to see Him come into His Kingdom.

Indeed, Jesus sat down on His throne 2,000 years ago. With that understanding "coming into His kingdom," we now, can look at our Lord's answer. As we look at this, do not jump to the conclusion that we reject a belief in the "Second Coming". We know that Jesus will return to earth at some point in the future, and we will talk about His "Second Coming" later when we look at our Lord's answer to the third question. What we are saying at this point is that the disciples' second question was not about Jesus' "Second Coming", but about His coming into His Kingdom.

Jonathan Edwards:

This is evident that when Christ speaks of his coming, his being revealed, his coming in his Kingdom, or his Kingdom's coming, He has respect to his appearing in those great works of his Power, Justice and Grace, which should be in the Destruction of Jerusalem and other extraordinary Providences which should attend it. (The History of Redemption, 1199, 1776. Dec. 1, 07,)

Jesus Answers the Second Question:

It is helpful to see how closely associated the destruction of Jerusalem was with the coming of Jesus into His Kingdom.

Jesus said: "But immediately after the tribulation of those days..." (Matthew 24:29) Jesus said that "immediately" after the destruction of Jerusalem, the disciples would know that He had come into His Kingdom.

He talks about that coming in the verse, which follows.

Matthew 24:30a: The Sign of The Son of Man

And then the sign of the Son of Man will appear in the sky. NASB

Futurist teachers look at these words and envision Jesus appearing in the sky. But look carefully. Does this verse say that Jesus will appear in the sky? It says that "the sign" will appear.

A sign is similar to a billboard declaring something.

What Is the Sign?

It is the sign of the Son of Man. It is not Jesus who will appear, but the sign will appear.

The King James Version of Matthew 24:30 reads like this:

"And then shall appear the sign of the Son of man in heaven."

Again, careful reading leads us to see that it is not Jesus who appears, but the sign that appears. And what will that sign indicate?

• That the Son of Man is in Heaven.
• He has arrived.

- He has sat down on His throne.
- He made it!

The King James Version refers to the Son of Man in "Heaven," while the New American Standard Bible (which we quoted earlier) refers to the Son of Man in the "sky."

Now get this: Either translation is correct because the Greek word ourano may be translated as either "heaven" or "sky."

However, if we use the word "sky," the reader may envision Jesus up above in the clouds. On the other hand, if we understand that Jesus is in "Heaven," then we may envision Him with His Father sitting on His throne.

It is this vision in Heaven that corresponds with Jesus' coming into His Kingdom.

- Put yourself in the shoes of the disciples 2,000 years ago sitting on the Mount of Olives.
- They soon were going to lose the One whom they had been follow- ing. He would die.
- After Jesus ascended into Heaven, how were they to know that He actually had made it into Heaven?
- How would they know that He had been given all authority over Heaven and earth?

That is precisely what Jesus was telling them. He was answering the question, "What will be the sign of Your coming into Your Kingdom?"

And What Is That Sign?

- Jesus had just told them about all the signs that would end in the destruction of Jerusalem and the Temple.
- That destruction was the sign.
- It was the billboard.
- Once they saw the destruction of Jerusalem and the Temple, they were to know without a doubt that Jesus Christ was on His throne in Heaven.

To gain an understanding of the impact that sign had on the first-century Jewish disciples, compare it with what happened to Japan in 1945 when two atomic bombs were dropped on Hiroshima and Nagasaki.

When those bombs decimated the two cities, Japanese people watching from a distance realized that the war was over. They had lost; and the United States had taken control.

Now compare that with what happened when Jerusalem was destroyed in A.D. 70.

- More people died in Jerusalem than when the two atomic bombs were dropped in Japan.
- The Jewish nation fell.
- The Temple was destroyed.
- That was the sign.
- When the Temple was destroyed, the Jewish religious system was ended.
- No longer could people approach God through the Temple with animal sacrifices.
- There was a new High Priest.
- The Stone that the builders had rejected had become the Chief Cornerstone.
- There was a new Temple being built out of living stones.
- That was the sign that Jesus came into His Kingdom.
- The throne of David had been lifted to heaven. From there Jesus Christ would rule over His eternal Kingdom.

Matthew 24:29: The Signs of Judgment

But immediately after the tribulation of those days THE SUN WILL BE DARKENED, AND THE MOON WILL NOT GIVE ITS LIGHT, AND THE STARS WILL FALL from the sky, and the powers of the heavens will be shaken. NASB

To fully understand this passage, first notice the time frame. Jesus said that these things would happen "immediately after the tribulation of those days." Since the tribulation that Jesus described happened in A.D. 70, we should look for the fulfillment of this verse "immediately" after A.D. 70.

To see this fulfillment, we need to be familiar with certain Jewish idioms.

The sun, the moon, and the stars frequently were used to refer to governing authorities. For example, Joseph had a dream in which the sun, moon, and stars all bowed down to him (Genesis 37:9); when Joseph relayed this dream to his family, they did not conclude that the sun, moon, and stars would literally bow, but that Joseph would be raised above governing authorities.

Similarly, we can read in Revelation 12:1 that a woman appears with the sun and moon under her feet and a crown of stars on her head, meaning that she had great authority.

In modern times we often use similar terminology when speaking of a movie star or a superstar.

In biblical terminology, the fame and glory of large cities were said to shine as the sun, moon, or stars.

When a certain city was destroyed, the sun, moon, or stars were said to darken.

For example, in the Book of Ezekiel we can read about the judgment and coming destruction of Egypt.

"And when I extinguish you, I will cover the heavens and darken their stars; I will cover the sun with a cloud And the moon will not give its light. All the shining lights in the heavens I will darken over you And will set darkness on your land," Declares the Lord God. (Ezekiel 32:7-8) NASB

This destruction that was prophesied by Ezekiel happened to Egypt, but there is no record of the sun, moon, and stars literally going dark. We can understand this more clearly when we realize that Prophets sometimes spoke in this apocalyptic terminology.

We can compare it with modern-day idioms that people may use when tragedy strikes:

- "His life caved in around him!"
- "They pulled the rug out from under him!"
- "The sky is falling!" or
- "It was lights out for him when he took that punch!"

It may be difficult for modern-day Christians to think of Jesus using such terminology, but that is exactly what He did. In fact, that is the only way we find this terminology used anywhere else in the Bible (as you will see in more examples listed below). It was a Jewish idiom in reference to coming destruction and the transfer of authority.

Consider how Isaiah decreed destruction upon a region south of Israel known as Edom: in Isaiah 34:4-5

> *And all the host of heaven will wear away, And the sky will be rolled up like a scroll; All their hosts will also wither away As a leaf withers from the vine, Or as one withers from the fig tree. For My sword is satiated in heaven, Behold it shall descend for judgment upon Edom And upon the people whom I have devoted to destruction.*

At that time in history the sky was not literally "rolled up like a scroll." The hosts of heaven did not literally fall to the ground as leaves from a fig tree. Yet, Edom was destroyed.

Finally, consider God's declaration of judgment through Isaiah upon Babylon. Isaiah 13:10

> *For the stars of heaven and their constellations Will not flash forth their light; The sun will be dark when it rises And the moon will not shed its light.* NASB

When Babylon Was Judged:

- There was no record of stars and constellations ceasing from shining.
- The sun was not dark when it came up.
- The moon did not dim. Yet destruction came.
- If we are going to allow the Bible to interpret itself, we will conclude that Jesus was using apocalyptic language to declare destruction.

Just as the Prophets Isaiah and Ezekiel spoke judgments against Egypt, Edom, and Babylon, so also Jesus as a Prophet declared destruction upon Jerusalem.

The disciples of Jesus would have recognized that phraseology. They knew the Old Testament. Such terminology was part of their cultural expressions.

This fits perfectly with what actually took place after Jesus died, was resurrected, and ascended into Heaven.

- Jesus sat down at the right hand of the Father.
- He was given all authority over Heaven and earth.
- The evidence on earth of Jesus ruling in Heaven was that the old Temple was destroyed.
- There was a new ruler: Jesus—the King of kings and the Lord of lords. Who is at the right hand of God, having gone into heaven, angels and authorities and powers had been subjected to Him. (1 Peter 3:22)
- The heavens were shaken because Jesus Christ came into His Kingdom.

Matthew 24:30b: The Son of Man in Glory

We have already examined the first part of Matthew 24:30; now let's consider the rest of the verse.

And then the sign of the Son of Man will appear in the sky, and then all the tribes of the earth [land] will mourn, and they will see the Son of Man COMING ON THE CLOUDS OF THE SKY with power and great glory. [Parenthesis belongs to the author] NASB

What is the meaning of "then all the tribes of the earth will mourn"?

To answer this, we need to examine the Greek word ge, which has been translated in this version to "earth." When this word ge is translated in other passages of the New Testament, it is most often translated as "land."

In fact, this word is often used when referring to the Promised Land of the Jews. This is what we believe is truer to the context of this passage. Hence, we are told that all the tribes of the land shall mourn.

Who Are the Tribes of The Land?

The land that is spoken of in this passage is the Promised Land. Therefore, all of the tribes of Israel will mourn.

When news of the destruction of the Temple and the whole of Jerusalem reached the tribes of Israel, great mourning took place in their synagogues and homes.

The "sign" (the destruction of Jerusalem) caused the "tribes" (of Israel) to mourn greatly, yet they still missed the significance of the sign.

It was the sign that "the Son of Man" was "in Heaven," that He had ascended to His Father.

When Jesus referred to "the Son of Man coming on the clouds of the sky with power and great glory," He did not say that the Son was coming back to earth. This event was to happen in the sky (or in heaven, according to the King James Version).

In Heaven Jesus was clothed with power and glory.

This is exactly what Daniel had prophesied as he saw in a vision Jesus Christ taking His position at the right hand of the Father: Daniel 7:13-14

I kept looking in the night visions, And behold, with the clouds of heaven One like a Son of Man was coming, And He came up to the Ancient of Days And was presented before Him. And to Him was given dominion, Glory and a kingdom, That all the peoples, nations and men of every language might serve Him. NASB

Daniel prophesied it. Then Jesus fulfilled it when He received the right to rule from His Father.

Matthew 24:31: Angels Gathering the Elect

And He will send forth His angels with a great trumpet and they will gather together His elect from the four winds, from one end of the sky to the other. NASB

To many people, this can speak only of the second coming of Christ at the end of history. But that is not what Jesus said it meant. Only three verses after this, He states: in Matthew 24:34-35

"Assuredly, I say to you, this generation will by no means pass away till all these things take place. Heaven and earth will pass away, but My words will by no means pass away."

Jesus said that this verse was descriptive of one of the things that would happen within the span of one generation. How can we understand this?

As Jesus sat down on His throne, all authority was given to Him in Heaven and earth.

- Everything changed the moment Jesus came into His Kingdom.
- The blowing of a trumpet meant to the Jews that a royal decree was going out. And what was that decree?
- It was time to release the angels of God to go and gather His people from every nation.
- At the same time, the disciples of Jesus were commissioned to go and preach the gospel, making disciples of every nation.

No longer was the Jewish nation the only people allowed within a covenant relationship with God. Jesus had become the Good Shepherd who was gathering His sheep from across the world.

Angels were to GATHER, His Elect...

The word "gather" is significant, for it literally means "to synagogue."

Christ's messengers would be gathering people together into His new synagogue.

The end of the old Temple would only help to hasten the building of the New Temple, which is the Church.

It is a simple fact of history that the Church began its vigorous growth after Jerusalem fell. After the Old Covenant Temple came down!

Matthew 24:32-33: Know That He Is Near

Now learn the parable from the fig tree: when its branch has already become tender and puts forth its leaves, you know that summer is near; so, you too, when you see all these things, recognize that He is near, right at the door. NASB

Jesus told the disciples here that just as the budding of a fig tree is a sure sign that summer is near, so also these warning signs would signal the beginning of a new spiritual season—the end of the old age and the flourishing of a new one.

Our Lord's lesson of the fig tree is even more powerful if we realize that Jesus and the disciples were sitting on the mountain, which overlooks Jerusalem and the Temple.

Our Lord could have easily taken a tender branch from a nearby tree and given them the lesson to watch for the obvious signs that would indicate the destruction of Jerusalem and His coming into His Kingdom.

Some teachers of the futurist view claim that the fig tree is a symbol of Israel and that when Israel is reborn as a nation, the generation that sees it happen will also see the Second Coming of Christ.

This is an astounding interpretation.

In the Bible, Israel typically is pictured as an olive tree rather than a fig tree (e.g., Jeremiah 11:16;)

The Lord called your name, Green Olive Tree, Lovely and of Good Fruit. With the noise of a great tumult, He has kindled fire on it, And its branches are broken.

And we know that this was referring to Israel as verses 1-3a records it:

"The word that came to Jeremiah from the Lord, saying, "Hear the words of this covenant, and speak to the men of Judah and to the inhabitants of Jerusalem; and say to them, 'Thus says the Lord God of Israel:'"

Romans 11:17

And if some of the branches were broken off, and you, being a wild olive tree, were grafted in among them, and with them became a partaker of the root and fatness of the olive tree,

Furthermore, there is no mention of a rebirth of Israel in this context.

Jesus already listed all of the signs for which they were to watch, and none of them implies anything about Israel being reborn.

In the context, Jesus was not talking about an event 2,000 years in the future. Jesus was answering His disciples' questions about His coming into His Kingdom—an event that they would see in their lifetime.

We can know that the fig tree illustration was not about the future rebirth of Israel and the Second Coming of Jesus because the next verse is the Lord's declaration that all of the signs would happen in that generation (Matthew 24:34 *"Assuredly, I say to you, this generation* [back then over 200 years ago, and not the 21st Century in which we live] *will by no means pass away till all these things take place."*) [Paraphrase and Emphasis Author's]

Furthermore, that would contradict what Jesus says two verses later (24:36 – *"But of that day and hour no one knows, not even the angels of heaven, but My Father only)* about there being no signs to indicate when His Second Coming would occur (a subject we will discuss shortly).

Jesus would not talk about looking at the obvious signs and then immediately say that He does not even know the day and the hour of His return.

For anyone who needs more proof, we can also know that the fig tree illustration was not about the rebirth of Israel and that generation seeing the Second Coming of Jesus, because it simply is not true!

Israel became a nation in 1948, and more than 67 years have passed without Jesus' return.

The obvious, simple lesson of the fig tree was to watch for all the signs listed in Matthew 24:4-28. When those signs were fulfilled, the disciples were to know that Jesus had come into His Kingdom.

Matthew 24:34: In This Generation

Jesus ended His answer to the disciples' second question by saying:

"Truly I say to you, this generation will not pass away until all these things take place."

If we take these verses literally, then we will believe that everything Jesus prophesied in Matthew 24:5-34 was fulfilled by A.D. 70.

Of course, futurist teachers cannot accept the words of Jesus.

Sometimes they redefine the word "generation" (genesis, in Greek) to be "race," and hence, they claim that all of the events listed in Matthew 24 will happen before the race of the Jews passes away.

In reality, that reinterpretation is inconsistent with the rest of the New Testament.

The Greek word genesis is used 34 times in the New Testament, and never is it translated as "race" in any commonly used translations of the Bible.

If we simply accept the natural and literal meaning of Jesus' statement, we will conclude that all of the events recorded, including the coming of the Lord, happened within the lifetime of the disciples who were listening to Jesus at that time.

Question #3: "What About the End of The World (Age)?"

The third question the disciples asked pertains to the end of the world (age) Matthew 24:3 KJV

And as he sat upon the mount of Olives, the disciples came unto him privately, saying, "Tell us, when shall these things be? and what shall be the sign of thy coming, and of the end of the world [age-KJV]?" [Parenthesis belongs to the author]

As we mentioned earlier, the Greek word for world, aion, is translated in some Bible versions as "age."

Jesus Answers the Third Question

Jesus answered the third question of the disciples in Matthew 24:36-25:46.

So here we go... Verses 36-44 No One Knows the Day or The Hour

But of that day and hour no one knows, not even the angels of heaven, but My Father only. But as the days of Noah were, so also will the coming of the Son of Man be. For as in the days before the flood, they were eating and drinking, marrying and giving in marriage, until the day that Noah entered the ark, and did not know until the flood came and took them all away, so also will the coming of the Son of Man be. Then two men will be in the field: one will be taken and the other left. Two women will be grinding at the mill: one will be taken and the other left. Watch therefore, for you do not know what hour your Lord is coming. But know this, that if the master of the house had known what hour the thief would come, he would have watched and not allowed his house to be broken into. Therefore you also be ready, for the Son of Man is coming at an hour you do not expect.

But of that day and hour no one knows—A question for you, what day and hour is being referred to here? From our previous study of the Scriptures, we can surmise that it refers to the day and hour that the Temple was going to be destroyed. The Old Covenant system was going to be dismantled.

It is like when a woman is pregnant; no one can give the exact day and hour of their delivery. Although some may have an idea of the month, no one really knows the exact time and hour. So even though Jesus had given some guidelines as to what they should look for they did not have an exact day and hour. And as Jesus rightly said, only the Father knew the exact time…

He then goes on to say—But as the days of Noah were, so also will the coming of the Son of Man be. As we have seen before this word or term "coming" means "parousia"

A Brief Note on Parousia

We are used to knowing this as "The Second Coming" of Christ (however, this is a phrase not found in the Bible) and is expressed by the Apostles in the following special terms:

"Parousia" (parousia), a word fairly common in Greek, with the meaning "presence". More especially it may mean "presence after absence," "arrival" (but not "return," unless this is established by the context of the text) for example, as in 1 Corinthians 16:17

I am glad about the coming of Stephanas, Fortunatus, and Achaicus, for what was lacking on your part they supplied.

2 Corinthians 7:6-7

Nevertheless God, who comforts the downcast, comforted us by the coming of Titus, and not only by his coming, but also by the consolation with which he was comforted in you, when he told us of your earnest desire, your mourning, your zeal for me, so that I rejoiced even more.

Philippians 1:26

that your rejoicing for me may be more abundant in Jesus Christ by my coming to you again.

And still more particularly it is applied to the Coming of Christ in the following thirteen passages:

1 Corinthians 15:23

But each one in his own order: Christ the firstfruits, afterward those who are Christ's at His coming.

1 Thessalonians 2:19

For what is our hope, or joy, or crown of rejoicing? Is it not even you in the presence of our Lord Jesus Christ at His coming?

1 Thessalonians 3:13

so that He may establish your hearts blameless in holiness before our God and Father at the coming of our Lord Jesus Christ with all His saints.

1 Thessalonians 4:15

For this we say to you by the word of the Lord, that we who are alive and remain until the coming of the Lord will by no means precede those who are asleep.

1 Thessalonians 5:23

Now may the God of peace Himself sanctify you completely; and may your whole spirit, soul, and body be preserved blameless at the coming of our Lord Jesus Christ.

2 Thessalonians 2:1

Now, brethren, concerning the coming of our Lord Jesus Christ and our gathering together to Him, we ask you,

2 Thessalonians 2:8

And then the lawless one will be revealed, whom the Lord will consume with the breath of His mouth and destroy with the brightness of His coming.

James 5:7

Therefore be patient, brethren, until the coming of the Lord. See how the farmer waits for the precious fruit of the earth, waiting patiently for it until it receives the early and latter rain.

James 5:8

You also be patient. Establish your hearts, for the coming of the Lord is at hand.

2 Peter 1:16

For we did not follow cunningly devised fables when we made known to you the power and coming of our Lord Jesus Christ, but were eyewitnesses of His majesty.

2 Peter 3:4

and saying, "Where is the promise of His coming? For since the fathers fell asleep, all things continue as they were from the beginning of creation."

2 Peter 3:12

looking for and hastening the coming of the day of God, because of which the heavens will be dissolved, being on fire, and the elements will melt with fervent heat?

1 John 2:28

And now, little children, abide in Him, that when He appears, we may have confidence and not be ashamed before Him at His coming.

—in all 13 times, besides
2 Thessalonians 2:9, where it denotes the coming of anti-Christ.

The coming of the lawless one is according to the working of Satan, with all power, signs, and lying wonders,

So, if we were to view this phrase for exactly what it means here in Scripture we must come up with a different understanding. So let me present this view to you:

What this verse is saying is that when this Old Covenant system was going to be put to death and the establishment of the New Covenant or Testament under Jesus Christ or that (His Coming or Parousia) would be established unbeknownst to anyone, but that there were certain signs that they could look for that would assist them in establishing what steps they could take as the time was very close upon them...

So let's read on ....Matthew 24:37-44 Jesus here was speaking to His 1st Century Apostles:

But as the days of Noah were, so also will the coming of the Son of Man be. For as in the days before the flood, they were eating and drinking, marrying and giving in marriage, until the day that Noah entered the ark, and did not know until the flood came and took them all away, so also will the coming of the Son of Man be. Then two men will be in the field: one will be taken and the other left. Two women will be grinding at the mill: one will be taken and the other left. Watch therefore, for you do not know what hour your Lord is coming. But know this, that if the master of the house had known what hour the thief would come, he would have watched and not allowed his house to be broken into. Therefore you also be ready, for the Son of Man is coming at an hour you do not expect.

Well, most futurist, end-time preachers have drilled into us that this is speaking of the rapture. Obviously, it could not be speaking of anything of that nature. So what exactly was it referring to? Does anyone have any understanding of what is being revealed here?

Again, remember that Jesus was speaking to His early Disciples over 2000 years ago. Not only that but they were all Jews and clearly understood what He was saying to them.

Also remember that in John 16:12-15, Jesus encouraging His Disciples about the coming Holy Spirit said this to them:

I still have many things to say to you, but you cannot bear them now. However, when He, the Spirit of truth, has come, He will guide you into all truth; for He will not speak on His own authority, but whatever He hears He will speak; and He will tell you things to come. He will glorify Me, for He will take of what is Mine and declare it to you. All things that the Father has are Mine. Therefore I said that He will take of Mine and declare it to you.

This passage really dovetails nicely into John's Revelation 1:1

The Revelation of Jesus Christ, which God gave Him to show His servants—things which must shortly take place. And He sent and signified it by His angel to His servant John,

Here we see the words spoken by Jesus taking full effect as John came into this Divine Revelation of the things that were soon to come to pass back in the 1st Century over 2000 years ago.

So here you have what I have researched, and you most certainly could do much further study in your times of private study and allow the Holy Spirit to bring greater light to you on this.

Verses 45-51, The Faithful Servant

Who then is a faithful and wise servant, whom his master made ruler over his household, to give them food in due season? Blessed is that servant whom his master, when he comes, will find so doing. Assuredly, I say to you that he will make him ruler over all his goods. But if that evil servant says in his heart, 'My master is delaying his coming,' and begins to beat his fellow servants, and to eat and drink with the drunkards, the master of that servant will come on a day when he is not looking for him and at an hour that he is not aware of, and will cut him in two and appoint him his portion with the hypocrites. There shall be weeping and gnashing of teeth.

Who then is a faithful and wise servant? And who then is the evil servant? Again, remember that Jesus was speaking to His early 1st Century Disciples and the Jews. Yes, the faithful servant referred to are His faithful followers and the evil servant was the disobedient 1st Century Jews.

You go on and read right into Matthew 25 without a chapter break, as the original manuscript did not have any chapter and verse... However, I believe what we have presented here would be enough for any serious student of God's Word to ponder deeply on what has been taught for many, many years and how it lacks thought and progression in context of what the Bible is saying and how it was written to the First Century Church. It is my opinion, that, if we were to truly read and study the Scripture, in its divinely ordered, First Century context, we would certainly come away with a similar understanding as I have presented here.[10]

And as we close the presentation of facts in this tome, remember this: The Italians have a saying, "traduttore, traditore." It literally means, "translator, traitor." Or more freely, "all translators are traitors."

So as one study the Word of God, there is much need to check and double check original words because if they are wrongly translated or interpreted, then, the result would be a wrong and inaccurate understanding of what was originally stated. This is why in order to grasp the truth behind the Scriptures, we need to study and delve deep into the sacred texts.

Ok, so now let us go back a bit to the first couple that was created by God, this is what He said to them:

Genesis 1:26-28

Then God said, "Let Us make man in Our image, according to Our likeness; let them have dominion over the fish of the sea, over the birds of the air, and over the cattle, over all the earth and over every

---

[10] For more on this subject, please see my book "Are We Living In The End-Times or Last Days". Get it here: https://www.amazon.ca/Are-Living-Times-Final-Days/dp/1486623174 or the eBook here: https://apostlemscantlebury.com/store/eschatology-a-biblical-view

creeping thing that creeps on the earth." So God created man in His own image; in the image of God He created him; male and female He created them. Then God blessed them, and God said to them, "Be fruitful and multiply; fill the earth and subdue it; have dominion over the fish of the sea, over the birds of the air, and over every living thing that moves on the earth."

Be fruitful and multiply; fill the earth and subdue it:

As I read this text some questions arose in my mind. For example, if we say this earth will come to an end, then, when are we to understand as the earth being filled with enough people, seeing that people are being born and are dying every day? At what point in time do we understand the earth as being subdued? Is it that God created the earth to eventually destroy itself, and if so when?

I would like to offer you the following thought, based on a few Scriptures:

Genesis 17:1-2, 7

When Abram was ninety-nine years old, the LORD appeared to Abram and said to him, "I am Almighty God; walk before Me and be blameless. And I will make My covenant between Me and you, and will multiply you exceedingly."

And I will establish My covenant between Me and you and your descendants after you in their generations, for an everlasting covenant, to be God to you and your descendants after you.

Jeremiah 32:40

And I will make an everlasting covenant with them, that I will not turn away from doing them good; but I will put My fear in their hearts so that they will not depart from Me.

Psalms 89:3-4

"I have made a covenant with My chosen, I have sworn to My servant David: 'Your seed I will establish forever, And build up your throne to all generations.' " Selah

From these Scriptures it seems that it is established that this world would continue forever, as the New Covenant has NO END DATE! Yes, I do know that this level of thinking would give some Saints serious problems. However, if you think that what I am suggesting here is unbiblical then you can reject it until you have given this some serious thought as my desire is to cause us to think!

In our next chapter we would be exploring the shinning of the Light on the Revelation.

Let's assess our understanding of Chapter Five: Shining The Light On Matthew 24 – II

1. What were the Jews expecting from their Messiah during the 1st Century?
2. Why was it that many who followed Jesus soon gave up and were quite vulnerable to predators who arrived on the scene claiming they were "Jesus"?
3. Which scriptures speak to the fact that there were imposters even at the time that the Apostles were preaching to the Early Church?
4. Do we have historical records of these happening, to back the biblical writings?
5. What is meant by the phrase "Pax Romana"?
6. What could have been the significance of Jesus's prediction of Wars and Rumors of Wars to His listeners?
7. Did Jesus's prediction come to pass during the lifetime of those to whom He was speaking – the 1st century believers?
8. Did Famines Occur during this time period? Explain with Scriptural Reference.
9. Did the earthquakes in Various Places take place as Jesus Predicted will take place soon—during the life span of those to whom He was speaking?
10. What was being birthed by ending the Old Covenant through the complete destruction of the Temple and that generation of Jews?
11. Did persecutions and tribulations, as predicted by Jesus, take place in the 1st Century?
12. How did John admonish the Early Church to decipher between the false prophets who were among them at the time of his writing?

13. According to Apostle John in 1 John 4:1-3 where were these false prophets operating?

14. Was apostle John then referring to the world as we know it today? Or to the world they were familiar with—their world which consisted of the Roman empire?

15. What were the false teachings that cropped up soon after?

16. Which scriptures speak to the fact that the Gospel was preached to the whole world in the 1st Century, as predicted in Matthew 24:14?

17. What are your thoughts on Apostle Paul's declaration of having the gospel being preached in "all creation under heaven" while he was still alive? Colossians 1:23

18. What is a clearer meaning to the Greek word "oikoumene" translated world in Romans 10:18 & Matthew 24:14?

19. After the Gospel was preached to the inhabited world as Jesus predicted, did the end of the world really come to pass? Explain

20. Why was the rebuilding of the Temple in AD 538 and its complete destruction in AD 70 of absolute significance to us today?

21. According to Jesus where are the true worshippers of God under the New Covenant expected to worship Him?

22. Do you agree that Jesus told His disciples in Matthew 24:15-20 that they need to be ready to flee "Judea" after they successfully preached the gospel to the whole world?

23. How can we know for a fact that Jesus' instructions to escape the end time destruction was specifically addressed towards the Jews and not the whole world as we know it today?

24. Did Jesus mention that the Abomination of Desolation standing in the Holy Place is to happen during the lifetime of His followers? Explain

25. What is your understanding of the Holy Place that is being referred to in Matthew 24:15-16; Luke 21:20-21 & Mark 13:14?

26. What was the Abomination of Desolation that Jesus was speaking of which was also spoken about by prophet Daniel?

27. Do historical records, of this time period, support the taking place of Jesus's prediction of "desolation of Jerusalem"?

28. Do you agree that Jesus' warning to flee Judea as soon as they see the armies surround Jerusalem was of utmost importance to have escaped the catastrophic events?

29. Why did Jesus call this "Great Tribulation" an occurrence such as had not occurred since the beginning of the world until now, or ever will."?
30. Where was Jesus' coming to happen according to Matthew 24: 27?
31. What is referenced by "the Corpse and Vultures" in Matthew 24:28?
32. Why was it necessary for God to bring to an end the Jewish identity and their religious system?
33. Which Scripture indicates to us the mindset that was prevalent among Jesus' disciples regarding His departure from earth?
34. What was the "coming" that the disciples were referring to when they questioned Jesus "What will be the sign of Your coming"?
35. Which Scriptures clearly state that the generation to whom Jesus was speaking will see Him coming into His Kingdom?
36. According to Jesus as recorded in Matthew 24:29, when was this "coming" to take place?
37. When He came into His Kingdom what was to appear in the Sky/ Heaven (translated from Greek ourano)?
38. Contrast the terminology in Matthew 24:29; Ezekiel 32:7-8; Isaiah 34:4-5; 13:10.
39. What is your understanding of Matthew 24:29?
40. Do you agree with the author that Matthew 24:30b is referring to "the all of the tribes of Israel" who will mourn?
41. Will you agree that Daniel's prophesy in Daniel 7:13-14 was fulfilled when Jesus ascended to Heaven and was handed the rulership of the Kingdom of God?
42. When was the Gathering of the Elect from the four winds to take place?
43. Who are elect that Jesus was referring to in Matthew 24:31?
44. Did this prophesy come to pass during the time period Jesus said it would? Explain
45. What signs did Jesus ask His followers to look for, in-order to know beyond the shadow of a doubt that the new era had begun under a New Covenant?
46. Which type of tree does God liken, the nation of Israel to, in Scripture?
47. Why is it not possible that Jesus was responding to the same question when He states "But that day and hour no one knows, not even the Angels of heaven, but My Father only"?

48. What day and hour was Jesus referring to in this portion of Scripture?
49. What does the Greek "Parousia" mean and is translated as, in the Bible?
50. Could this word "Parousia" mean "coming again" unless it is established by the context?
51. Who are being referred to as faithful and evil servants in Matthew 24: 45-51?
52. What was God's assignment to the first man and woman as stated in Genesis 1:26-28?
53. Will we ever be able to know if we have completely filled the earth or subdued it?
54. What did God promise to Abram as a reward for his faithfulness, to walking upright and blameless before Him?
55. Is it possible that God truly meant "everlasting" as in this earth would continue forever, generations to come—world without end?

CHAPTER SIX
SHINING THE LIGHT ON THE REVELATION

WE UNDERSTAND THAT THE BOOK OF REVELATION WAS WRITTEN BACK IN THE first Century to a first Century Church and not to a 21st Century Church. Here is a document written by Dr. Cindye Coates and used by permission to reveal this fact.

[11]The Dating Of The Book Of Revelation

Dr. Cindye Coates

We are about to see why it is essential to interpret Scripture with Scripture vs. interpreting Scripture with Heresy and Traditions. With the dating of Revelation, we establish the true historical prospective. If we date it early, you have its fulfillment with God's judgment on the Old Covenant Israel. If we date it late, we have every man's idea. So dating plays a very important part in its interpretation. There are differences of opinion as to when this book was written. These can be summed up as the "late date" and the "early date" theories. First, we'll cover the late date theory. Then we'll examine the facts which support the early date theory.

THE LATE DATE THEORY

Those who hold to the "late date," have Revelation written during the time of Domitian Caesar (AD 95-96). This date is determined by the following statement by Irenaeus (AD 130 to AD 202), as quoted by Eusebius, the church historian, in AD325:

---

[11] Dr. Cindye Coates; Author - "The Fulfilled Prophecies of Jesus www.PresentTruthMatters.com

"We will not, however, incur the risk of pronouncing positively as to the name of Antichrist; for if it were necessary that his name should be distinctly revealed in this present time, it would have been announced by him who beheld the apocalyptic vision. For that was seen not very long time since, but almost in our day, towards the end of Domitian's reign."—Irenaeus

There are things about this statement that need to be noted:

First, Irenaeus did not witness this. He referred to Polycarp (who supposedly knew the Apostle John).

Secondly, the key part—"it is not long since it was seen"—is ambiguous. According to Irenaeus recollection, Polycarp saw "it" sometime in AD 95-96, during the last part Domitian's reign.

Thirdly, we do not know if the "it" Polycarp was referring to was John, the visions he saw, the name of anti-Christ, or the book itself and we do not know if he meant that the book was written at that time or not. Furthermore, it comes to us through three people separated by three centuries. Simply put, this is hear-say. This statement, even with all of this uncertainty, is the only evidence used to support the "late date" theory. It has been accepted by generations of people without really questioning it or examining it in light of the Bible itself. The late date has been passed on to us in the same way it was passed on to Eusebius; it [was] handed down by tradition. Tradition is not the way to interpret Scripture.

Another statement by Irenaeus seems to indicate the earlier date also. In his fifth book, he speaks as follows concerning the Apocalypse of John and the number of the name of the Antichrist: "As these things are so, and this number is found in all the approved and ancient copies." Domitian's reign was almost in his own day, but now he speaks of the Revelation being written in ancient copies. His statement at least gives some doubt as to the "vision" being seen in 95 AD which was almost in his day, and even suggests a time somewhat removed from his own day for him to consider the copies available to him as ancient.

THE EARLY DATE THEORY

So, where can we turn to find evidence for the dating of Revelation? Within the book itself! Let Scripture interpret Scripture! It will be shown, from internal evidence that Revelation was written before the destruction of Jerusalem in AD 70.

(1) JOHN'S AGE - HE MUST PROPHESY AGAIN...

The first point to consider in favor of the early date is the fact that John was told that he "must prophesy again before many peoples, and nations, and tongues, and kings" in Revelation 10:11. Now, if Revelation was written in AD 95-96,John would have been over 90 years old and it would have been very difficult for him to travel to the various "nations and... many kings" and preach. However, with Revelation written earlier, John would have been in his mid-60's and at that age, his traveling would have been more feasible.

(2) THE SEVEN CHURCHES IN ASIA

Another point is that John wrote Revelation to a specific group of churches in Asia (Revelation 1:4). The importance of this statement cannot be overlooked (even though it has been by many scholars).

There is only one small window of time in which there were only seven churches in Asia. The early AD 60's. The apostle Paul established 9 churches in that area, but only 7 were addressed in Revelation. The reason for this is that the cities of Colosse, Hierapolis, and Laodicea, were all destroyed by an earthquake around AD 61. Laodicea was rebuilt soon afterwards, but the other two cities were not. This left only seven churches in Asia during the five years just prior to the beginning of the Roman/ Jewish war in AD 70.

Of particular importance is the message to the church of Philadelphia (Revelation 3:7-13). In versus 10 and 11, Christ told John to inform them that an "hour of temptation" was "about to come upon all the world," i.e., the Roman Empire. Christ then told them that He was coming quickly and that they should hold fast. The reason this is important (besides the fact that this was directed to an actual church in the First Century) is that the first persecution of Christians took place under Nero Caesar in AD 64. Therefore, Revelation must have been written before that time.

(3) THE TEMPLE WAS STILL STANDING

One of the most compelling proofs that Revelation was written before Jerusalem was destroyed is the fact that the Jewish temple was still standing!

Revelation 11:1-2, "And there was given me a reed likes unto a rod: and the angel stood, saying, Rise, and measure the temple of God, and the altar, and them that worship therein. But the court which is without the temple leave out, and measure it not; for it is given unto the Gentiles: and the holy city shall they tread under foot forty and two months."

How do we know that this was the temple of the First Century and not some future one? First, there is not one verse in the entire Bible that speaks of a "rebuilt" Jewish Temple. Not one. That alone should be proof enough.

However, this passage is very similar to Luke 21:20-24. Notice that Jesus told the disciples that they would see this event. They had asked Him about their temple (verse 5), and Jesus told them it would be destroyed before their generation passed away (verse 32). Notice again what Jesus said in verse 24, "Jerusalem shall be trodden down of the Gentiles." This is the same thing Christ told John in Revelation 11:2. Therefore, since the disciples' generation has long since passed away, Revelation must have been written before the nations trampled Jerusalem underfoot in AD 70.

(4) THE TRIBES OF THE EARTH

Most writers consider the theme of the book to be Revelation 1:7. This verse is very similar in context to Matthew 24:30.

Revelation 1:7,

"Behold, he cometh with clouds; and every eye shall see him, and they also which pierced him: and all kindreds [Greek word #5443] of the earth shall wail because of him. Even so, Amen."

Matthew 24:30,

"And then shall appear the sign of the Son of man in heaven: and then shall all the tribes [Greek word #5443] of the earth mourn, and they shall see the Son of man coming in the clouds of heaven with power and great glory."

It may not be conclusive standing alone, but you can see that just based on the language, a case can be made that the two verses are speaking of the same event. Matthew 24:30 is a verse that speaks of the fall of Jerusalem. And that is just the case that I am making about the Book of Revelation—it speaks of the fall of Jerusalem in AD 70.

Notice also the language of Revelation 1:7. It speaks of those who "pierced him." Although we know that the Romans crucified him and pierced him, the apostles accused the Jews of the act. In Acts 2:23,36, Peter says that they crucified Jesus. He continues to state this in his following sermons (Acts3:15; 4:10; 5:30). Stephen, in Acts 7:51-52, calls them murderers. And Paul, in 1 Corinthians 2:8, speaks of the Jews killing the Lord. And also in I Thessalonians 2:14-15, he speaks of the Jews that killed both the Lord Jesus and the prophets. So perhaps the book concerns itself with the Jews.

This view is further reinforced with the phrase, "kindreds of the earth." ("kindreds" is from the Greek word *phule*, which means "tribe"). This is a direct allusion to the Jewish tribal system.

Now, we must identify, from Scripture, who those "tribes" were. To do that, we must keep in mind this simple rule of interpreting the Bible: let Scripture interpret Scripture. We can do that quite easily by looking at Zechariah 12:10-14.

Zechariah 12:10-14,

"And I will pour upon the...inhabitants of Jerusalem, the spirit of grace and of supplications: and they shall look upon me whom they have pierced, and they shall mourn for him, as one mourneth for his only son...In that day shall there be a great mourning in Jerusalem...And the land shall mourn, every family apart; the family of the house of David apart, and their wives apart; the family of the house of Nathan apart, and their wives apart; The family of the house of Levi apart, and their wives apart; the family of Shimei apart, and their wives apart; All the families that remain, every family apart, and their wives apart."

Obviously, this is the foundation for John's statement that "every eye shall see him, and they also which pierced him: and all kindreds of the earth (or land) shall wail because of him" So, in essence, Zechariah was saying that the "tribes of the land" would mourn for Him whom they had pierced. Who were those tribes? "The inhabitants of Jerusalem." This also helps us identify the "earth" in Revelation1:7. According to Zechariah, the "earth" is the land of Palestine, specifically, Jerusalem. Also, it is those tribes, i.e., the nation of Israel, who would "look upon Me whom they have pierced." And because of that, "the mourning in Jerusalem" would be great. With all of this information, we can see that the "tribes of the earth" in Revelation 1:7 are the nation of Israel. The "earth" is Palestine. The land that would mourn is Jerusalem.

So, the main purpose of Revelation would be to reveal Jesus to the nation of Israel. The place of this revealing would be Jerusalem. Lastly, this revealing would be to those who pierced Him, i.e., the Jews. This is not a general reference to the Jewish nation, but to Christ's contemporary generation. That generation was destroyed in AD 70, by the Roman Legions. Therefore, the Book of Revelation must have been written before that event.

(5) THE WOMAN

The next thing that we need to look at is "the woman" found in chapters 17 and 18. John wrote that he saw a "woman drunken with the blood of the saints, and with the blood of the martyrs of Jesus" (17:6). The "woman" had this name written on her forehead: "MYSTERY, BABYLON THE GREAT, THE MOTHER OF HARLOTS AND ABOMINATIONS OF THE EARTH" (17:5). The angel said that "the woman" was a poetic symbol of "that great city" (17:1; in whom "was found the blood of prophets, and of saints, and of all that were slain upon the earth." (18:24). Then John wrote, "Rejoice over her, thou heaven, and ye holy apostles and prophets; for God hath avenged you on her... Thus with violence shall that great city Babylon be thrown down, and shall be found no more at all." (18:20, 21). So who was this "woman?" This "great city?"

John gave us a clue in Revelation 11:8, where he wrote, *"And their dead bodies shall lie in the street of the great city, which spiritually is called Sodom and Egypt, where also our Lord was crucified."* This shows us, as we saw above, that John was referring to the Jerusalem of his day.

To prove this assertion, let's look at the term "Sodom." John wrote that this is a "figurative" name. That means it does not tell us the actual name of the city, but it's spiritual condition. Once more, in letting the Bible interpret itself, we find this is a reference to Jerusalem. In Isaiah, chapter 1, after declaring that he had a "vision...concerning Judah and Jerusalem" (verse 1), Isaiah wrote, "Hear the words of the Lord, you rulers of Sodom." In Jeremiah 23:14, because of the adulterous prophets, God said that Jerusalem and her inhabitants were "all of them unto means Sodom."

But what about "Egypt?" Nowhere in the Bible is Jerusalem called Egypt. However, the first century generation was also in an exodus. While Old Testament Israel's exodus was from the bondage of Egypt, the New Testament Israel's exodus was from the bondage of the Old Covenant Law. The most recognizable passage that depicts this "new exodus" is found in I Corinthians10:1-11. Paul wrote, *"Now all these things happened unto them for ensamples: and they are written for our admonition, upon whom the ends of the world are come."* His contextual foundation for this statement was the Old Testament exodus from Egyptian bondage. He wrote that they had passed through the sea (verse 1). They ate manna and drank from the rock (verse's 3-4). He then relays how they wandered in the wilderness (verse 5), became idolaters (verse 7), tried the Lord and were destroyed by serpents (verse 9). This shows us that, just like the "type and shadow" of the Old Testament and their deliverance from bondage, the New Testament saints were undergoing the same exodus. The only difference was that Paul's generation was the reality to which the Old Testament example pointed.

Furthermore, in Luke 13:33-34, Jesus said, *"[Today and tomorrow, and on the following day], I must travel on, because it is not possible [for] a prophet to perish outside Jerusalem. Jerusalem! Jerusalem! The [one] killing the prophets, and stoning those having been sent to her."* Then, in Matthew 23:29-37, Jesus blasted the Jews of His day for killing the prophets and the apostles. He declared that they are the children of their fathers who also killed the prophets. Then in verse 32, Jesus said that they would complete the sin that their fathers started. But the most crucial evidence is found in verse 35, where Jesus said, "upon you (i.e., the Jews of His day) may fall the guilt of all the righteous blood shed on the earth." Then He said, "I tell you the truth, all of these things will happen to you people who are living now. Jerusalem, Jerusalem! You kill the prophets and stone to death those who are sent to you" (verse's 36-37). In both passages, Jesus told the Jews of His day that they were guilty of "all the righteous blood shed upon the earth"(see also Acts 7:51-52).

Therefore, since both of these passages deal with the same crime and the same judgment, the "great city" of Revelation must be the Jerusalem of Christ's generation. Which further proves that Revelation was been written before Jerusalem fell in AD 70.

(6) THE SIXTH KING—"NERO" REVELATION 17:10

And there are seven kings: five are fallen, and one is, and the other is not yet come; and when he cometh, he must continue a short space.

So far we have seen that Revelation deals with the revealing of Jesus to First Century Israel. As noted above, "the woman" John saw was First Century Jerusalem. The "kings," therefore, were the rulers of the known world of John's day, i.e., the Roman Empire. The "kings" were not ruling at the same time, for the text stated, "five fell," meaning that five of those kings had come and gone. Then "one is," meaning the "king" who was ruling at the time Revelation was written. Here in this verse, we have one of the clearest proofs for dating this book. If we simply examine the list of Roman Emperors, we will be able to determine who the sixth king was, and the time Revelation was written.

Here are the Roman Emperors:

(1) Julius Caesar

(2) Augustus

(3) Tiberius

(4) Gaius (Caligula)

(5) Claudius

~ «five fell» ....

(6) Nero

Nero reigned from 54AD to June of 68AD. (*Galba to follow who reigns but six months.) Here we find the terrible persecutors of the Christians (at whose hand Peter and Paul were martyred), whom God used to destroy the apostate Jews. Nero was in power and he gave the command to Vespasian to destroy Jerusalem. This was the 6th king, proving beyond any doubt that Revelation was written before the Roman/Jewish war.

Historically, Nero is the one that persecuted Christians beyond all comparison. St. John's banishment to Patmos was itself a result of the great persecution of Nero. The apostle Paul was tortured and then beheaded by the evil Emperor Nero at Rome in A.D. 67. The apostle Peter, who was crucified upside down, was another victim of Nero.

(7) THE SONG OF MOSES

To anyone familiar with the Law of Moses and Jewish tradition, Revelation 15:2,3 will have meaning. It says that those martyrs "who had come off victorious from the Beast" were singing "the Song of Moses."

Question:

If these martyrs are Christians living 2,000 years after Christ, why would these Christians be singing the Song of Moses? Does any Christian alive today know how to sing this song? Deuteronomy 32:1-43 is the song that John has reference to.

The Jews were to sing this song to remind themselves of what would befall them "in the latter days" (***Deuteronomy 31:29***). The song talks about "their end"—the Jews (verse 20), and details their destruction by a consuming "fire" (verse 22), "famine"(verse 24), "plague" (verse 24) and "bitter destruction" (verse 24). God calls them a "perverse generation" (verses 5 and 20), and says He will "render vengeance" upon them and "vindicate His people" (verse 41 and 36 respectively). Why would Christian martyrs of the 21st century be singing this song about the Romans, when the song had reference to the Jews living in the 1st Century? It wouldn't make much sense.

Aren't these the same martyrs who cried out earlier, "How long, O Lord, wilt Thou refrain from judging and avenging our blood" (Revelation 6:10)? Who was it who had all the "blood of the righteous" martyrs imputed against them? Clearly, it was Christians who had kept their faith in Jesus, in spite of the intense persecution, and "had come off victorious from the Beast." (See Matthew 23:35 and Luke 13:33)! This passage (Revelation15:2,3) points very clearly to followers of Christ living in the First Century.

In Revelation 16:10,11, it says that the people in the Beast's kingdom "gnawed their tongues because of pain." They had great sores on their bodies along with other plagues that had been poured out on them. We know from Josephus when the Jews literally gnawed their tongues for lack of food during the siege of AD 70! And, it is interesting that Josephus even calls the Jewish Zealot forces a "wild beast" in several places (Wars V.1.1; IV.7.4; IV.9.8; V.2.5)! This point is emphasized even more by the fact that the whole context of the Song of Moses is full of references to "beasts," "serpents," and "dragons" (Leviticus 26; Deuteronomy 28-32; Deuteronomy 32:24,33).

(8) THE TIME ELEMENT

Next consider the expectations of the author, Jesus Christ. He tells John to expect the fulfillment of the prophecy **soon.** (Revelation 1:1,3; 2:16; 3:11;22:6,7,10,12,20).

In Revelation 1:1,3, right off the bat, John informed his readers, the seven churches of Asia (verse 4), that the contents of this volume **"must shortly come to pass."** Please note, that John did not write that some of the events, or even most of the events must shortly take place. He wrote that **all of the events** contained in Revelation «must shortly come to pass.» Why? Why must those things «shortly come to pass?» Because «**the time (was) at hand."** At hand for whom? The seven churches of Asia, specifically, and to the church of the First Century in general. The time for what was at hand. "The Revelation of Jesus Christ." Remember, as we saw above, this is the main episode of Revelation.

In Revelation 22:6, John wrote that the Lord sent an angel to John "to shew unto his servants the **things which must shortly be done."** Here, at the end of the book of Revelation, John recorded the exact same message that he did in chapter 1. This again **emphasizes that all of the events contained in Revelation were about to take place in the First Century**—not stretched throughout time, and certainly not for any future generation.

In Revelation 22:10, the angel of the Lord said to John, *"Seal not the sayings of the prophecy of this book: for the time is at hand."* Once more, we have proof that the events of Revelation were about to **take place in the First Century**. However, another element was added to this warning. The angel told John not to seal the Scroll. Why is this important? To answer that, let's look at the book of Daniel.

After Daniel had received visions concerning his people (the nation of Israel), he was told, **"thy people shall be delivered, every one that shall be found written in the book"** (12:1). Daniel is then told how they would be rescued—by resurrection, some would be rewarded with **"everlasting life"** and others with "everlasting contempt" (verse 2). But then, Daniel is told something very peculiar. In verse 4, **Daniel was told, «shut up the words, and seal the book, even to the time of the end.** Please note that this verse says the **"time of the end", and not "the end of time"**. There is a huge difference between the end of time and the time of the end. Now, we must ask "**Whose time of the end?"** Verse 1 told us that **Daniel's visions concerned the nation of Israel**, not mankind in general.

Next, Daniel saw two angels talking about the fulfillment of all that he had seen (verse 6). One asked the other, **"How long shall it be to the end of these wonders?"** The answer was, **"when he shall have accomplished to scatter the power of the holy people, all these things shall be finished."**(verse 7). But Daniel could not understand what they meant, so he asked again, "When?" The angel answered, **"Go thy way, Daniel: for the words are closed up and sealed till the time of the end."**(verse 9). Now that we have looked at this passage, how does it relate to Revelation 21?

Did you know that there is only one other place in the Bible where a sealed book is referred to? Revelation, chapter 5. How Daniel relates to Revelation is that Revelation is the opening of Daniel's sealed book!! Remember, Daniel's visions were concerning the **"time of the end" of Israel**, and Revelation is about God's judgment on apostate Israel. They are one and the same. The reason this has direct bearing on Revelation 21, is that Daniel was told to seal his book concerning the end **"for it pertains to many days in the future" (Daniel 8:26), but John was told not to seal his book «because the time is at hand» (Revelation 22:10)**. The end of Old Covenant Israel and the Law of Moses was coming to an end. The age of Grace had arrived to which there would be no end.

All things written had to be fulfilled by the time Jerusalem fell in AD 70 (see Luke 21:20-22). Therefore, since Revelation is the opening of Daniel, then it must have been fulfilled by the summer of AD 70.

Our next time statement is found in Revelation 22:12. There, Jesus told John, **"And, behold, I come quickly;** and my reward is with me, to give every man according as his work shall be." Notice that **Jesus did not say that "when I come, I will come quickly,"** He emphatically said that He was coming **"quickly."** But He also said something else. He said that His reward was with Him to give every man according to his works. **Now some state that this has not happened yet. However, we must let Scripture interpret Scripture, and turn to Matthew 16:27-28 and Mark 8:38-9:1 and Luke 9:26-27.** Jesus said the exact same thing in these three verses that He did in Revelation 21.

In Revelation 21, He said He was coming and "he shall reward every man according to his works." These are the exact same "comings" with the exact same "rewards." But, Jesus also said in these three verses, **"There be some standing here, which shall not taste of death, till they see the Son of man coming in his kingdom**." Notice that Jesus tied His coming to the lives of His disciples. **He said that some of his listeners would not die until He came.**

But to whom is He coming? And what will be their reward? **Jesus said that the "coming" would be to the first century generation of Israel (Matthew 24:34, Mark 13:30, Luke 21:32). Daniel told us that the" rewards" would be that some would be resurrected to "everlasting life" and others to "everlasting contempt".** Now, let's put these two passages together. Jesus said He was coming and He was going to reward each according to his works, and that some of the disciples wouldn't die until they saw this take place. Therefore, since all of the first century disciples are dead, Jesus must have returned and rewarded each according to his works. Furthermore, in Revelation, He said the same thing, therefore it must be fulfilled!

CONCLUSION

If a person doesn't believe the first three verses of Revelation (the near expectation of the events), neither will he believe the rest of the book. For if a person is unwilling to accept the time constraints of the text, the rest of the document can mean anything that the reader desires.

If the Apostle John was banished to Patmos under the reign of Nero, as the internal evidence indicates, **he wrote the book of Revelation about AD 68 thru 69. Nero committed suicide in AD 68.** One of the oddest facts about the New Testament is that the single most datable and climactic event of the period—the fall of Jerusalem in A.D. 70—is never once mentioned as a passed fact!! This means it had not happened yet and the Book of Revelation is a warning about the «soon» and «near» event that was about to occur.

The inscription to the book of Revelation, in the Syrian version, first published by Deuteronomy Dieu, in 1627, and, afterwards in the London Polyglot, is the following, **"The Revelation which God made to John the evangelist, in the Island of Patmos, to which he was banished by Nero Caesar." This places it before the year of our Lord 69 AD.**[12] **(End of article)**

---

[12] Dr. Cindye Coates; Author - "The Fulfilled Prophecies of Jesus www.PresentTruthMatters.com

I would also like to submit the following script concerning the dating of the Revelation, so that we could get a very clear understanding as to the date of its writing:

DATING THE REVELATION (PARAPHRASED FROM DR. JOHN NOE)

The actual moment in time when the book of the Revelation was given to John the Apostle on the isle of Patmos is of critical importance in unlocking its mysteries. Unfortunately, scholars have reached different conclusions after assessing the dating evidence. The majority contends for a date around A.D. 95 or 96. This date is termed the "late date." But a sizeable and growing minority feels the Revelation was written prior to the destruction of both the Temple and the city of Jerusalem's in A.D. 70. This is termed the "early date."

I believe that adherence to the late date effectively rules out any contemporary and significant historical event as the soon-coming fulfillment or any relevance for its original and named recipients [those to whom this book was specifically written to, although it holds great significance to us here living in the 21st Century. Especially as many Believers today are still looking for a 'rapture' to occur and an anti-christ to manifest. Both leading to an incorrect interpretation of the Scriptures]. However, with the acceptance of the early date, this opens the possibility that it describes those events leading up to and including Jerusalem's fall and the destruction of the Temple in A.D. 70.

Notably, Philip Schaff, who wrote *History of the Christian Church* in eight volumes, and in the Preface to his Revised Edition, admits that "on two points I have changed my opinion – the second Roman captivity of Paul . . . and the date of the Apocalypse (which I now assign, with the majority of modern critics, to the year 68 or 69 instead of 95, as before)"[13]

Most interestingly, a major piece of dating evidence cited by the popular late-date theorists is an ambiguous and questionable passage written by Irenaeus, one of the early Church fathers who wrote around A.D. 180-190. But translation difficulties, precludes this passage from being used as evidence. Moreover, Irenaeus said nothing about the date of the writing of Revelation. The bigger issue with Irenaeus, however, is his credibility. He claimed that Jesus' earthly ministry lasted approximately fifteen years and that Jesus lived to be almost fifty years old. Thus, the

---

[13] (Philip Schaff, *History of the Christian Church*, Vol. 1, (Grand Rapids, MI.: Eerdmans, 1910 [third revision]) *vi*, also 420, 834n).

difficulties with Irenaeus' writings in this dating matter are many and varied.

On the other hand, and in our opinion, arguments for the early date are superior, both quantitatively and qualitatively, to those advanced for the late date. For example, of the two types of dating evidence, scholars generally acknowledge internal evidence (contained inside a document) as preferable and taking precedence over external evidence (what others, like Irenaeus, have said about a document).

John A.T. Robinson in his book *Redating the New Testament* points out that Revelation, along with all New Testament books, says nothing about the destruction of Jerusalem and the Temple in A.D. 70. He terms this omission as "one of the oddest facts," and questions why this event "is never once mentioned as a past fact" by any New Testament book, even though it is "predicted" and "would appear to be the single most datable and climactic event of the period" (John A.T. Robinson, *Redating the New Testament* (Philadelphia, PA.: Westminster Press, 1976) 13).

This omission propelled Robinson's re-dating study. His hypothesis and eventual conclusion was that "the whole of the New Testament was written before 70." He places the writing of Revelation in A.D. 68 (Ibid., 10, 352). Admittedly, Robinson's argument is an argument from silence. But those who claim that Revelation was written in AD 95-96 do have major difficulties explaining this omission.[14]

[15]WHEN WAS IT OR WILL IT BE FULFILLED?

The book of Revelation does not contain end-of-the-world predictions or events, as is commonly held. Rather, it fully predicted and described, symbolically and accurately, the events leading up to and including the fall of Jerusalem in a coming of the day of the Lord, in judgment, and in the change of covenants, in A.D. 70. All this and more occurred "soon" and "shortly"—i.e., within two to seven years, depending upon the exact date of this book's writing. Any interpretation of its fulfillment that lies beyond the time frame of its original hearers and readers is, at best, suspect.

Again, first and foremost, the book of Revelation described a local series of events very near to its writing and intended for an original and

[14] https://www.prophecyrefi.org/our-teachings/book-of-revelation/when-was-it-most-likely-written/
[15] https://www.prophecyrefi.org/our-teachings/book-of-revelation/when-was-it-or-will-it-be-fulfilled/

primary audience. These all occurred. Mistakenly, however, many feel that these events were only local and not worldwide. But just like the birth, life, death, resurrection, and ascension of Jesus, which were also local events, the Revelation's fulfillment has universal applications and implications. Locally is just how God is choosing to fulfill it and his plan of redemption.

These events ended, forever, biblical Judaism, its age, and the Old Covenant system (Hebrews 8:13; 9:10).

Reluctantly, the late, renowned, and futuristic theologian George Eldon Ladd conceded that "there must be an element of truth in this approach, for surely the Revelation was intended to speak to its own generation" (Ladd, *A Theology of the New Testament*, 672). Mistakenly, however, he and many others feel that if this prophecy is totally fulfilled, this makes it meaningless to modern-day Christians. But as we are about to see, Revelation's past fulfillment does not exhaust its meaning, relevance, and symbolism. In fact, just the opposite is true. Past fulfillment makes this prophecy *more meaningful*, not less. Why? It's because the Revelation is more than a tract for its own times. How can we know this? It's not some doctrine we have dreamed up, which leads us to our fifth foundational key for unlearning many popular misconceptions and unlocking the mysteries of this vital book.

AUDIENCE RELEVANCE

So, as we study the Word of God, we must use this master key—Audience Relevance. And we do this by asking a few questions such as:

1. To whom was this passage or letter written to?
2. Why was it written?
3. How did those to whom it was written understood it?
4. Then we can ask—how does this apply to me? How could I benefit from it?

And I am sure that there are other questions that can be asked. However, this is a good place to begin. You would gain much more from your time of study as you do!

As we continue, I would like for us to visit the first and last chapters of the book [its bookend if you will] of Revelation. However, before doing so let us take a look at the name of this letter. Remember the title for this letter "The Revelation" is translated from the Greek language, the language it was originally written in. The Strong's concordance reveals that the Greek word used is the word apokalypses, pronounced (ä-po-kä'-lü-pses) meaning:— appearing, coming, lighten, manifestation, be revealed, revelation.

It was written as a disclosure of truth and instruction concerning divine things which were once unknown — especially those relating to Christian salvation—given to the soul by God Himself, or by the ascended Christ, especially through the operation of the Holy Spirit (1 Corinthians 2:10 *"God has revealed to us through the Spirit. For the Spirit searches everything, even the depths of God."*).

In order to be distinguished from other methods of instruction as stated in Ephesians 3:3 *how the mystery was made known to me by revelation, as I have written briefly."* It was a spirit received from God disclosing what and how great are the benefits of salvation as per the following outlined in Ephesians 1:17.

That the God of our Lord Jesus Christ, the Father of glory, may give you a spirit of wisdom and of revelation in the knowledge of him,

Let us now look at the first and last chapters of the book of Revelation:
Revelation 1:1

The Revelation of Jesus Christ, which God gave Him to show His servants—things which must shortly take place. And He sent and signified it by His angel to His servant John,

Revelation 22:20-21

He who testifies to these things says, "Surely I am coming quickly." Amen. Even so, come, Lord Jesus! The grace of our Lord Jesus Christ be with you all. Amen.

[16]Much of the conflict and confusion over the Revelation stems from just such a practice of taking part or all of this prophecy out of its

16 Dating the book of Revelation: John Noe, The Greater Jesus: His glorious unveiling (pp. 97-98, 104). East2West Press. Kindle Edition. (Paraphrased)

divinely determined time context, stretching it like a rubber band by nineteen centuries and counting, plopping it down out into the future, and creating a pretext for its fulfillment. But disregarding or abusing context is not the prerogative of any sincere reader or honest interpreter.

The Book of Revelation places its own direct and contextualizing time statements upon the whole of its prophecy. Like bookends at its beginning and end (its first and last chapters/introduction and conclusion/prologue and epilogue), these time statements establish the historical framework for the soon and now past fulfillment of the whole prophecy.

These bookends to the book of Revelation gives us the urgency of the message contained in this book to its original readers. It also reveals to us who is the Source of the revelation contained in this book. In the opening verse we read that it is the Revelation of Jesus Christ, which God gave Him to show to His servants. And then the final verse of this book reveals that once again Jesus declares to the original readers over 2,000 years ago *"Surely I am coming quickly."*

The strategic placement of these bookends brackets the entire prophecy and was done, no doubt, to avoid confusion. So, from this we know that what is contained in the revelation of this book had very significant meaning to its first recipients—the First Century Believers.

But most commentators and prophecy teachers have missed, dismissed, or ignored these time and contextualizing statements, as well as their strategic placement:

- *"what must soon [shortly] take place"* (Revelation 1:1; 22:6 [KJV]).
- *"Blessed is the one who reads the words of this prophecy ... who hear it and take to heart [obey] what is written in it"* (Revelation 1:3; 22:7 [KJV]).
- *"the time is near [at hand]"* (Revelation 1:3; 22:10 [KJV]).
- *"Do not seal up the words of the prophecy of this book"* (Revelation 22:10). Note: Daniel was told to *"close up and seal the words"* of his book *"until the time of the end"* (Daniel 12:4). In the Revelation, that time was now *"near"* or *"at hand."*
"Behold, I am coming soon [quickly]!" (Revelation 22:7, 12 [KJV]).
- *"Yes, I am coming soon [quickly]."* (Revelation 22:20 [KJV]).

Once again, these full-content-bracketing time statements establish the immediate historical context for the fulfillment of the whole of the prophecy. When ignored, as so many have done, it's easy to lose sight of the proverbial "forest for the trees." (*End of paraphrase*).

What is needed is a careful, honest, and consistent approach—one that preserves the integrity and harmony of the whole of the prophecy and its associated events. Arbitrary divisions and specialized or alternative meanings of common and ordinarily understood words have no part in this process. The simplest solution is to recognize that the whole of the prophecy was written, first and foremost, to 1st Century Christians.

Now there are basically four views people use for revelation when reading the book of Revelation that I would like for us to explore before going forward: Idealism, Futurism, Historicism, and Preterism. Each of these views of interpretation answer the basic four questions—when, how, why, and where—very differently.

Paraphrased from Jonathan Welton's book "The Art of Revelation"

To understand this, let's imagine four experts standing in front of the Book of Revelation, and each expert has been trained by one of these four schools of thought. A passerby joins the group of experts and begins to ask the four important questions in hopes of understanding this book.

He begins with the first question: "When was this book written?" The Preterist responds first. "It was likely painted during the reign of Nero, based on the prophecy about seven kings listed in Revelation 17. It was written regarding the AD 70 destruction of Jerusalem, and as a prophecy of that event, it was written in advance of that event."

Then the Idealist, Futurist, and Historicist chime in together. "It doesn't really matter when it was written," they say, "because the content is prophetic. It is probably about distant events and mysterious symbols.

The novice then introduces his second question, "How was this book written?" he asks. "What reasoning and understanding did the writer use?" Once again, the preterist quickly speaks, saying, "Revelation was written in the same manner as the books of Ezekiel, Jeremiah, and Isaiah, which all describe the first destruction of Jerusalem in 586 BC. John chose this style because of the AD 70 destruction of the temple."

The other three nodded in mild agreement, and then voice their differences. "We do agree that Revelation is full of Old Testament symbolism and imagery, yet we definitely do not agree that John wrote it this way because of the AD 70 destruction of the temple."

The Idealist adds, "John chose these symbols to point to the ongoing spiritual cosmic struggle between the kingdom of darkness and the kingdom of light, in which light ultimately wins." "I'd say, instead, that he cloaked all of Church history in mysterious symbolism centuries before it would unfold as it has and continues to unfold," the Historicist says.

Finally, the Futurist adds his point of view. "I agree that there are symbols and Old Testament references, but I believe that it will all make sense someday in the future when these events begin."

"All this is very interesting," the novice says. "But why did the writer pen this book?" This time, the Historicist chimes in first. "John was compelled to write all of human history into one book. He penned it in advance of all the major coming events, centuries ahead of time. This has always been the nature of prophecy."

The Futurist shook his head, saying, "I believe John was transported in a vision to the distant future, and when he returned from his vision, he recorded all that he witnessed about the time of the end of human history."

After quietly thinking for a few moments, the Idealist says, "I disagree with you both. John was a very mystical man. We see this from his strange Gospel account, which is so very different from the other three. I believe John wanted to show the cosmic struggle and the victory of Jesus in grand splendor."

At last, the Preterist speaks. "I keep telling you guys, the Early Church was surviving under brutal persecution, and in that context, John said his writing was understandable (Revelation 13:18) and a blessing (Revelation 1:3; 22:7) to those who saw it. If his writing was about the distant future or served as an overlay of Church history, how would this encourage them? I believe the Christians in the First Century knew exactly what John's writing meant."

"Ok. I can see the four of you don't agree on much," says the novice, chuckling. "Perhaps you can give me an answer to my final question: Where was the book written? What location does it reference?"

"The Revelation," says the Idealist, "represents the heavenly realm and is written with all the spiritual pictures and components expected of a story about the battle between light and darkness."

"I disagree," says the Futurist. "The location referred to in the Revelation is the planet earth in the future."

The Historicist then adds his perspective. "The location isn't so important, considering that this has been unfolding and will continue to unfold over time. Although the city with seven hills is probably Rome, (Revelation 17:9) and Babylon the Harlot is probably the Roman Catholic Church."

The Preterist answers last, saying, "The numbers, dimensions, measurements, and specifics that are recorded in the Revelation all made perfect sense to First Century Christians. There was very little mystery to the imagery that John used to convey his message to his intended audience. Only as the dust of Church history has settled has this writing become more mysterious."

The other three stare in disbelief at the Preterist, who always seemed to be proposing the most unusual ideas. Our bystander novice smiles and thanks his expert friends.

"Clearly," he says, "there are four different ways to look at this writing. Now I will have to decide which one I like the best."

This imaginary dialogue gives us a basic understanding of each of these viewpoints. In the next chapter, we will examine the answers to the bystander's four important questions more closely. These questions are the key to helping us see the big picture of Revelation. [End of paraphrase]

The Latest Picture of Jesus

The first chapter of the Book of Revelation (the Apocalypse) unveils and reveals the latest and only full-blown, physically descriptive picture of Jesus in the Bible. By inspiration, John records what he heard and saw when Jesus literally and physically came, appeared, touched, spoke to, and commissioned him on the island of Patmos over nineteen hundred years ago:

I, John, your brother and companion in the suffering and kingdom and patient endurance that are ours in Jesus, was on the island of Patmos because of the word of God and the testimony of Jesus. On the Lord's Day I was in the Spirit, and I heard behind me a loud voice like a trumpet, which said: "Write on a scroll what you see and send it to the seven churches: to Ephesus, Smyrna, Pergamum,

Thyatira, Sardis, Philadelphia, and Laodicea. I turned around to see the voice that was speaking to me. And when I turned I saw seven golden lampstands, and among the lampstands was someone "like a son of man," dressed in a robe reaching down to his feet and with a golden sash around his chest. His head and hair were white like wool, as white as snow, and his eyes were like blazing fire. His feet were like bronze glowing in a furnace, and his voice was like the sound of rushing waters. In his right hand he held seven stars, and out of his mouth came a sharp double-edged sword. His face was like the sun shining in all its brilliance. (Revelation 1:9-16)

Make no mistake; this is Jesus as He is now! We are not told the meaning of the sword coming out of his mouth or why his hair is white and his eyes like blazing fire. Nor are we told why a crown of thorns no longer encircles his head. But one thing is sure. He is no longer the Jesus of popular thought and tradition. He is that of course, but He is now much more. Grasping the full reality of this divinely revealed and new image of Jesus and knowing and serving Him as He is today, and as He requires, are essential prerequisites if we hope to hear the words someday, *"Well done, good and faithful servant"* (Matthew 25:21, 23; Revelation 1:3; 22:7). Anything less is less.

But tell me, where is this image of Jesus being presented, nowadays? Where is this picture of today's Christ hanging on a wall? Where is this present-day and pertinent perspective being taught, studied, and worshiped? Since the time John personally saw and experienced Jesus like this, Jesus has not changed. Therefore, we can definitely affirm that *"Jesus Christ is the same yesterday and today and forever"* (Hebrews 13:8). That is, He is the same in his Personhood and Divinity—the Second Person of the Trinity.

Critical Objection: Some theologians contend that the word "yesterday" means Jesus has never changed from His pre-existence before creation and ever since.[17] That assertion, however, is only partially true as William Hendriksen properly explains: "He is the same Saviour, yet different from the days of his humiliation."[18] The Greek word translated

---

[17] The Greek word translated "yesterday" is chthes. For its two other uses, see John 4:52 and Acts 7:28. Hebrews 13:8 is literally correct as it reads.
[18] William Hendriksen, *More that Conquerors* (Grand Rapids, MI.: Baker Book House, 1940, 1962, 1982), 56.

"yesterday" is chthes. For its two other uses, see John 4:52 and Acts 7:28. Hebrews 13:8 is literally correct as it reads. William Hendriksen, More than Conquerors (Grand Rapids, MI.: Baker Book House, 1940, 1962, 1982).

I would like you to see and understand what I am about to say before going forward: Jesus always existed within His Eternal Father, who has no beginning or end, He is Eternal, always was and always will be. The natural earthly Jesus as the Son of God had a beginning and an end. As you would recall He was born of the virgin Mary who was impregnated by God's Holy Spirit. So, there is a natural, earthly dimension to Jesus. There is no denying this, but we have to understand that He is not like that anymore and that is not the Jesus we need to worship. This Jesus was necessary to enter the earth realm and become the Saviour of humankind, because we all know or should know that God will not use any other form to work through upon the earth. When He created Adam, God set the stage for the one through whom He would work in the earth realm.

After Adam and Eve gave up their birthright to the devil God worked through the ages to get a perfect man that He could work through, but He could not find any because all were born in sin and shaped in iniquity. It was not until He decided to come in the Person of His Son Jesus the Christ to live a perfect human life and then to willingly go to the Cross and lay down His life for the sins of the human race did God finally find the Perfect man He desired. However, this same Jesus after He rose from the grave came into His pre-human manifested form into His true image that we must now worship as the Christ, Jesus the Son of the Living God. Once again here is His eternal description: Revelation 1:10-16

I was in the Spirit on the Lord's day, and I heard behind me a loud voice like a trumpet saying, "Write what you see in a book and send it to the seven churches, to Ephesus and to Smyrna and to Per'gamum and to Thyati'ra and to Sardis and to Philadelphia and to La-odice'a." Then I turned to see the voice that was speaking to me, and on turning I saw seven golden lampstands, and in the midst of the lampstands one like a son of man, clothed with a long robe and with a golden girdle round his breast; his head and his hair were white as white wool, white as snow; his eyes were like a flame of fire, his feet were like burnished bronze, refined as in a furnace, and his voice was like the sound of many waters; in his right hand he held seven stars, from his mouth issued a sharp two-edged sword, and his face was like the sun shining in full strength. (Emphasis Author's)

I submit to you that this is the Jesus as He was yesterday, today, and forever. Yes, the historical Jesus is very important, but we don't need to worship Him like that anymore. He finished His human assignment and has stepped back into His eternal place with the Father. Are you seeing this?

I would now like to explore a statement in Revelation 22:12-15

"And behold, I am coming quickly, and My reward is with Me, to give to every one according to his work. I am the Alpha and the Omega, the Beginning and the End, the First and the Last." *Blessed are those who do His commandments, that they may have the right to the tree of life, and may enter through the gates into the city. But outside are dogs and sorcerers and sexually immoral and murderers and idolaters, and whoever loves and practices a lie.*

As I read this a few questions rose in me:

1. When He said 'behold, I am coming quickly,' where was He coming to?
2. They would have access to 'the tree of life', where is this 'tree of life'?
3. The gates of the city, seems to be referring to a place on planet earth. And outside those gates are the 'dogs and sorcerers and sexually immoral and murderers and idolaters, and whoever loves and practices a lie.'

Now, if that is so, this will prove to us that this world will not end, according to a couple passages of Scripture, in the King James Version: Isaiah 45:17

But Israel shall be saved in the LORD with an everlasting salvation: ye shall not be ashamed nor confounded world without end.

Ephesians 3:21

Unto him be glory in the church by Christ Jesus throughout all ages, world without end. Amen.

In our next chapter, we will explore the Light that was created on day one.

Let's assess our understanding of Chapter Six: Shining The Light On The Revelation.

1. Do you concur with Dr. Cindye Coates' statement "dating plays a very important part in the interpretation of the Revelation"? Why?
2. According to the "late date" theorists, when was the Revelation written?
3. What credible evidence is used to support this theory?
4. According to the "early date" theorists, when was the Revelation written?
5. What evidence is used to support this "early date" theory & how credible are they?
6. What is the Greek word #5443 that is translated tribes/kindreds?
7. Do you agree with the author's statement: "So, the main purpose of Revelation would be to reveal Jesus to the nation of Israel. The place of this revealing would be Jerusalem. Lastly, this revealing would be to those who pierced Him."? Explain.
8. Who do you believe is the "woman" that is referred to in Revelation Chapters 17 & 18?
9. How does the seven kings mentioned in Revelation 17:10 contribute towards assessing the time "Revelation" was written?
10. Do you know the Song of Moses? Will this be the song that would come to your mind if you were to come out victorious from any kind of martyrdom?
11. To whom was the Song of Moses relevant?
12. Do you agree that Revelation 15:2-3 was referring to the Jewish Christian martyrs and not Christians 2000+ years later?
13. In Revelation 22:10, the angel instructs John not to Seal the book unlike in Daniel 12:4 where he instructs Daniel to seal the book even to the time of the end. Why do you think this was?

14. From Daniel 12:1 can we glean whose time of the end Daniel was prophesying about?
15. Can we prove that Daniel's visions concerning the "time of the end" of Israel and Johns vision in Revelation are both prophesies about the same event?
16. In your opinion is there enough compelling evidence to believe that the Revelation was written before AD 70 when the Jewish "World" came to an end with the complete destruction of the Old Covenant Temple and Rituals?
17. What did Jesus tell John about His coming in Revelation 22:12?
18. If you were to parallel Revelation 22:12 with Matthew 16:27, Mark 8:38-9:1 and Luke 9:26-27 do you agree that Jesus specifically says that there would be some of them who were standing there at that time, 2000+ years ago, will see Him come in His Glory?
19. So, could this have been talking about our generation today or several after us when this event is going to take place?
20. Do you agree that the book of Revelation is a warning about the "soon" and "near" event that was to occur in their generation (1st Century) and not in ours?
21. When studying Scripture, why is it important for us to use the master key—Audience Relevance?
22. What does Jesus Christ who is enthroned in heaven look like?
23. Why is it important for us to get to know Him as He is today?
24. What is the Greek work translated "yesterday" in Hebrews 13:8? What does it mean?
25. How else is this same word translated in John 4:52 & Acts 7:28?
26. Why was it necessary for Jesus to enter the earth in the human form?
27. Do you agree with the author's statement: "Now, if that is so, this will prove to us that this world will not end, according to a couple passages of Scripture"?

Chapter Seven
THE LIGHT CREATED ON DAY ONE

Genesis 1:1-5

In the beginning God created the heavens and the earth. The earth
was without form, and void; and darkness was on the face of the
deep. *And the Spirit of God was hovering over the face of the waters.* Then God said, "Let there be light"; and there was light. *And
God saw the light, that it was good;* and God divided the light from
the darkness. God called the light Day, and the darkness He called
Night. So the evening and the morning were the first day. (Emphasis Author's)

So, here we read the account of the creation of Day and Night on the
first day that God arrived on planet earth, which He had obviously created before. This is so because the record began with this statement: *In
the beginning God created the heavens and the earth.* As to when that beginning was we have no record. However, we do know that something
occurred between when God created the heavens and earth and when
He revisited it in verse two. Again here is what it said in Genesis 1:2 The
earth was without form, and void; and darkness was on the face of the
deep. *And the Spirit of God was hovering over the face of the waters.*

I offer to you the following: we just do not know how old the earth
is based on this record and that lucifer and one third of the angelic host

rebelled against God, and were cast down to earth and they disrupted the order that God had established when He had first created the earth. And we draw this conclusion because of several facts about God.

- God is Light and in Him there is no darkness, according to 1 John 1:5 *This is the message which we have heard from Him and declare to you, that God is light and in Him is no darkness at all.*
- As we read through the creation account we see this aspect of God shining through. Let me give you the account of the next five days: Genesis 1:6-10

Then God said, "Let there be a firmament in the midst of the waters, and let it divide the waters from the waters." Thus God made the firmament, and divided the waters which were under the firmament from the waters which were above the firmament; and it was so. And God called the firmament Heaven. So the evening and the morning were the second day. *Then God said, "Let the waters under the heavens be gathered together into one place, and let the dry land appear"; and it was so. And God called the dry land Earth, and the gathering together of the waters He called Seas.* And God saw that it was good.

- Genesis 1:11-13

Then God said, "Let the earth bring forth grass, the herb that yields seed, and the fruit tree that yields fruit according to its kind, whose seed is in itself, on the earth"; and it was so. And the earth brought forth grass, the herb that yields seed according to its kind, and the tree that yields fruit, whose seed is in itself according to its kind. And God saw that it was good. So the evening and the morning were the third day.

- Genesis 1:14-19

Then God said, "Let there be lights in the firmament of the heavens to divide the day from the night; and let them be for signs and seasons, and for days and years; and let them be for lights in the firmament of the heavens to give light on the earth"; and it was so. Then God made two great lights: the greater light to rule the day, and the lesser light to rule the night. He made the stars also. God set them in the firmament of the heavens to give light on the earth, and to rule over the day and over the night, and to divide the light from the darkness [here we see God creating two lights to give light to the earth, after He had called forth Light on Day one]. And God saw that it was good. So the evening and the morning were the fourth day.

• Genesis 1:20-23

Then God said, "Let the waters abound with an abundance of living creatures, and let birds fly above the earth across the face of the firmament of the heavens." So God created great sea creatures and every living thing that moves, with which the waters abounded, according to their kind, and every winged bird according to its kind. And God saw that it was good. And God blessed them, saying, "Be fruitful and multiply, and fill the waters in the seas, and let birds multiply on the earth." So the evening and the morning were the fifth day.

• And on the sixth day He created mankind: Genesis 1:26-27, 31

Then God said, "Let Us make man in Our image, according to Our likeness; let them have dominion over the fish of the sea, over the birds of the air, and over the cattle, over all the earth and over every creeping thing that creeps on the earth." So God created man in His own image; in the image of God He created him; male and female He created them.
   Then God saw everything that He had made, and indeed *it was* very good. So the evening and the morning were the sixth day.

So, from this creation account it is clear to see that our God is Light and that darkness cannot be associated with Him. That darkness is the realm that satan operates in. And yes, he at times masquerade as an angel of light, but that is only a part of his deception.

Hence the reason the first thing that God did on Day one of His visit to the earth He had previously created, was to say, **"Let there be Light."** He reestablished the order He established in His creation.

Another question that I asked as I saw this, was: What was that Light for? As it was not to light the day. I offer this: First of all it was a "spiritual Light" and it is in one sense, similar to our Creator; unseen to the natural, earthly eye, hence the reason for creating lights on day four. Adam and Eve were to live in that LIGHT, as God would have come down and fellow-shipped with them (Genesis 3:8). I believe it is similar to the realm that we step into once we are saved and baptized in the Holy Spirit today. We step into that LIGHT, unseen but very, very real!

As we bring this book to a close, there is another 'puzzling' command given to the first couple that I am seeking light on. It is here in Genesis 1:26-28 King James Version:

> *And God said,* Let us make man in our image, *after our likeness: and let them have dominion over the fish of the sea, and over the fowl of the air, and over the cattle, and over all the earth, and over every creeping thing that creepeth upon the earth.* So God created man in his own image, in the image of God created he him; male and female created he them. And God blessed them, and God said unto them, Be fruitful, and multiply, and <u>replenish</u> the earth, and subdue it*: and have dominion over the fish of the sea, and over the fowl of the air, and over every living thing that moveth upon the earth.* [Emphasis Author's]

Here we see God creating man and woman and then giving them this command: Be fruitful, and multiply, and <u>replenish</u> the earth.

When would that command be fulfilled? Seeing people are dying en masse every day while babies are being born en masse every day at the same time. Is there going to be a cutoff point to this?

- •The word replenish means: to make full or complete again, as by supplying what is lacking, used up, etc..
- • To replenish one's stock of food. to supply (a fire, stove, etc.) with fresh fuel. to fill again or anew.

My question then is: what did God have in mind as to the replenishing of the earth and if so when and how would we know when this is so? Maybe this leads to the idea of the world never having an end from the beginning, hmmm?

It is my prayer that the teachings of this book would add value to your life, and that the Holy Spirit will guide you as you seriously consider what is shared in these pages. I speak Kingdom Blessings over you and thanks for taking the time to study what I have presented here.

Let's assess our understanding of Chapter Seven: The Light Created on Day One

1. Do we have an account of when God created the earth?
2. What did God do on Day One when He was hovering over planet earth?
3. On which day did God create the greater and lesser lights to govern the day and night?
4. Can we then agree that the light that God called forth on Day 1 and the Light as we know which proceeds from the Sun and moon are different?
5. Do you see, as 1 John 1:5 reveals to us that God is light and there is no darkness in Him at all?
6. So why then would it have been that the heavens and the earth that He created was found without form and void and in darkness?
7. While God operates in the realm of light, are we aware of who operates in the realm of darkness? Explain with scripture.
8. What is the light that God called forth on Day 1?
9. What was God's command to Adam & Eve in Genesis 1:28?
10. In your opinion have we accomplished this as a human race? Have we fully replenished the earth and subdued it?
11. What yardstick can we use to measure our progress?

OTHER EXCITING TITLES
BY MICHAEL SCANTLEBURY

THE RESURRECTION OF THE DEAD ONES

What happens to a person when they die? It is one of the most asked and least understood questions in all of life and for the Christian, it entails the idea of a resurrection. Every Christian denomination—and there are many—believe one simple truth: the tomb was empty after the crucifixion of Jesus. We often hear sermons where the focus is on the cross and the resurrection is mentioned only in passing. But when you really get into the meat of the Word of God, the Bible clearly shows that the resurrection of Jesus was the gospel message preached by the Apostles and not the Cross.

Sadly, the Believers only seem to get excited about the resurrection once a year at Easter time. In reality, every Sunday should be Resurrection Sunday. The early Church met on the first day of the week to celebrate Jesus' defeat of death. Imagine the impact from consciously gathering every week to celebrate the resurrection...

And in that vein, we need to seek to arrive at a clear biblical understanding of this particular question regarding what happens to a person when they die. It is my earnest prayer that we, together, could arrive at a much better understanding of this subject.

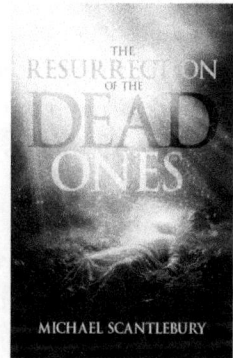

NAVIGATING THROUGH SPIRITUAL TRANSITIONS

We are all in transition. It's a natural phase of life for us. Transitions can take many forms, as I am sure you've experienced yourself.

Transitions build stories and reveal the history of our lives. They happen whether you desire them to or not. There is no way around them unless you are dead. So, if you are choosing life, anticipate and prepare for transitions. They are coming and will come again.

According to the dictionary, a "transition" is **a Movement, Passage, or Change from One Position to Another.** The word "transition" is often used in human services to refer to the general process of someone moving, or being moved, from one set of services or circumstances to another.

As Christians, each transition period we go through, God is leading us to ensure that we come into the fullness of all that He has promised in and through our local houses/churches. This leading He does with the many local houses/churches across the earth that are also experiencing various transition periods! However, I believe that there are dangers to be aware of in this journey as we stride towards our destiny.

Every leader regardless of his or her calling in life will experience seasons of transition. We make the common assumption that once we've arrived at a certain place that we are beyond being tested. It is not so! Those who serve closest to a leader when in transition must know how to stick in both good and bad times. Times of certainty and times of uncertainty.

It is my earnest prayer that this book will aide you in your times of transition!

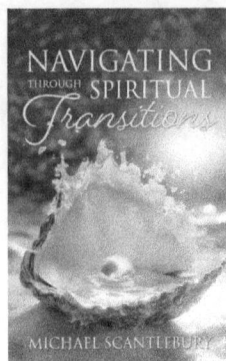

EXPLORING THE SECRETS OF HIDDEN WEALTH

This masterpiece, has been quite controversial in some quarters, the subject of finances in the Kingdom. In his usual straight forward but yet biblical approach, Apostle diligently explained the parables of Jesus in view of provisions, delving into a strong theological framework for stewardship and how to form relevant

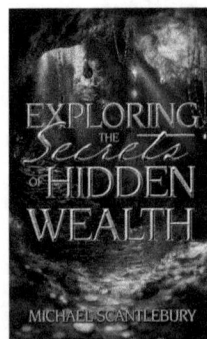

partnership for wealth which is an effective interaction with the world system for material advance and contentment as a Kingdom virtue.

This book served to fuel in us an even deeper personal search into God's intention for wealth among His people. It provides a unique perspective on God's heart towards us and His empowering ability, through resources, to bring His purpose to pass.

"Exploring the Secrets of Hidden Wealth" is a revelatory guide to understanding the power, purpose and stewardship of money.

GOD'S ETERNAL PLAN

Let me quote this very important passage of Scripture: Hebrews 11:1-3

> Now faith is the substance of things hoped for, the evidence of things not seen. For by it the elders obtained a good testimony. By faith we understand that the worlds were framed by the word of God, so that the things which are seen were not made of things which are visible.

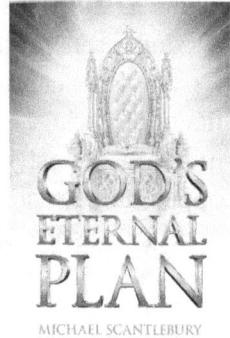

So, this is the premise from which this book would be written. We cannot even begin to understand the Scriptures or the heart of God if we do not believe that He is. And to do that we must enact the faith that everyone of us were given at birth according to: Romans 12:3

Because God always existed, we must understand and believe that He existed outside of space and time in the realm called *Eternal*. I believe that this is why we could understand the following passage of Scripture: Matthew 25:34-40

So, He knew exactly what He was seeking to accomplish, and nothing could take Him by surprise.

And that *time*, as we know it only began when He created it. This was done when He created the Heavens and the earth as recorded in the book of Genesis, when He established the sun and the moon and day and night causing, the establishment of days and night, and the record of days.

UNDERSTANDING THE DUAL ASPECTS OF FAITH
From the onset, Apostle Scantlebury presents the tenets of his tome, by eloquently contrasting the two dimensions of Faith: (1) where we use our Faith to acquire and believe God for new things and victories in Him and (2) where we use that same Faith to resist and battle against all odds that is thrown at us.

After defining the elements of faith, Apostle Michael empowers us with the tools to increase our faith: Our knowledge of God and the application of what we know. It's not enough to know what the Word of God says. What produces real faith is displayed when our actions match our belief.

Apostle Scantlebury gives us an accurate understanding of the benefits of our trials. Contrary to our Westernized belief, Faith and trials are mutually inclusive. We are encouraged to keep trusting God despite the opposition. Trusting God then becomes the substratum of having a pleasant relationship with Him.

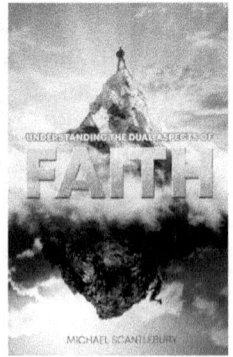

UNDERSTANDING THE REVELATION
As we embark on this study, there are certain things that we need to first establish. Here are five things that I believe the book of Revelation is about:

1. Revelation is the most Biblical book in the Bible.
2. Revelation has a system of symbolism.
3. Revelation is a prophecy about imminent events – events that were about to break loose on the world of the First Century.
4. Revelation is a worship service.
5. Revelation is a book about dominion.

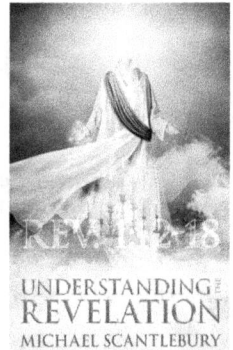

Also, we have to study The Revelation as a part of the entirety of Scripture and not as a separate book on its own. It ties in beautifully with the rest of the Bible and Israel's journey. So, as we study the prophecy within this book, we will see how it ties in with Jesus' prophecy recorded in Matthew 24 and many of the words spoken directly to the tribes of Israel. It was a powerful and very relevant book for the First Century Church and gives us today a clear picture of God's way of dealing with His people. When approached from this point of view, fresh realms of understanding will herald some fresh and powerful truths for us today.

Also, we need to bear in mind that the Bible is a record of Two Covenants; the Old Covenant which had a shelf life and was destined to come to an end. And then we have the New Covenant which is eternal and as such will never end. It has been eternally established by our King and Lord, Jesus the Christ. We need to add to this the understanding that the entire cannon of Scripture was written prior to AD 70.

ARE WE LIVING IN THE END TIMES OR THE LAST DAYS?

Whenever we hear this term "end-times or last-days" it conjures up all kinds of images in our minds: from the universe blowing up with the largest flames you could ever imagine! And that it would usher in a new heaven and a new earth. We also have presupposed in the body of Christ that before all of this would indeed occur, the righteous would be raptured away and then the world would be left a massive fire of destruction.

When you hear Christians mention the 'last days,' many just assume it's referring to the end of time and of the world. But the attentive Bible student asks, 'last days of what?' It seems obvious to me that the text is referring to the end of the Old Covenant-Temple aeon/age. When you read the New Testament through these lenses, all I can say is WOW! It makes a significant difference, when you read the Scriptures with the realization that the Bible was written FOR you and not TO you.

We need to also understand that "time of the end" and "end of time" are not one and the same thing. The Bible teaches about the "time of the end" but there is nothing taught about an "end of time."

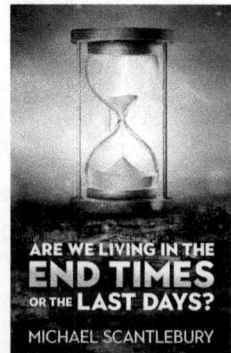

FATHERS AND SONS – AN UNVEILING

As we embark upon this study, there is something that I would like for us to first understand, and it is this: God the Father is the ultimate Father. There has never been anyone like Him, nor is there currently anyone like Him, nor will there ever be anyone like Him. He is in a class all by Himself.

Another thing that we need to understand moving forward is this: Respect produced by force and domination is not respect but fear.

Also, when we speak of sons, we are not only referring to the male gender, but we are speaking of **a new class in God**. Those that have been washed by the Blood of Jesus and have entered the New Covenant with Him. Notice that in the Scriptures, it never states "Sons and Daughters of God."

John 1:12 states

But as many as received him, he gave them power to be made the sons of God, to them that believe in his name. ...

As such, I do believe that women can also be Apostles and in a broader scope, they qualify to "father" should that mantle be upon them.

HEAVEN & EARTH A BIBLICAL UNDERSTANDING

Whenever we today in this 21st Century read about heaven and earth in the Scriptures we need to be careful as to exactly what is being referred to. And here are some reasons as to why this must be.

1. The original Bible was not written in our modern English, which is a far different language than Hebrew and Greek the original languages of the Holy Scriptures. Hence the reason for us to become avid students of the Word of God.

2. We, living today are not the original recipients of Scripture and as such we need to understand what the original recipients understood when they first received that Word.

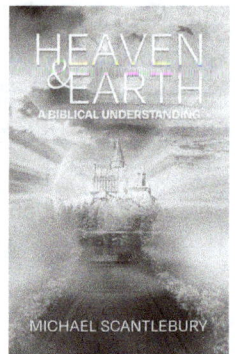

3. We must be willing to let the Bible interpret itself and not hang on to our theories for the Scriptures.
4. That the Bible speaks of at least four Heavens and three earths. And as such we need to dig deep into the Word of God and find them and apply this understanding in our study.

Remember what the Scriptures say in Proverbs 25:2 *It is the glory of God to conceal the word, and the glory of kings to search out the speech.*

With that said let us now take a deeper dive and journey into the Word of God with the intention of extracting much needed revelation concerning these Heavens and Earths.

MY PONDERINGS

In this book before you the author has been engaged in pondering several subjects and as such, decided to put his thoughts in a book. As you read through these pages may the Lord use his thoughts to both inspire and bless you. Here are some of the subjects he has been pondering, with each one making up a chapter of this book:

My Ponderings on The Kingdom of God
My Ponderings on The Church
My Ponderings on Innovation
My Ponderings on Wisdom and The Power of Vision
My Ponderings on Navigating Seasons
My Ponderings on Breakthroughs
My Ponderings on Unity
My Ponderings on The Many Comings of Jesus
My Ponderings on Eschatology
My Ponderings on Jesus the First Fruit of the Dead
My Ponderings on Understanding the Times
My Ponderings on Understanding the New Covenant
My Ponderings on Gold

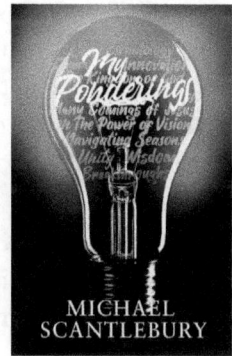

UNDERSTANDING THE KINGDOM OF GOD AND THE CHURCH OF JESUS CHRIST

"This book is a game changer and will teach you what it means to be part of This Kingdom."

Pastor Marilyn Bailey
—Teleios Church, Johannesburg,
South Africa

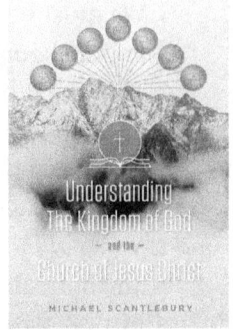

"There is perhaps no greater time to revisit the spiritual and practical understanding of the kingdom of God than right now.

Apostle Scantlebury addresses and corrects, common misconceptions, explains the contrasts in the Kingdom of God and the kingdom of darkness, properly aligns the Kingdom and the Church, and propels us toward a holistic understanding of Kingdom life in the earth.

With great patience and clear articulation, Apostle Scantlebury lays out a compelling case for the people of God to give priority to understanding and walking in the principles of the Kingdom of God in life and ministry.

Do yourself a favour; set aside some time to read through and study this transformative volume. You will be challenged, changed, and equipped to be a proper representative of the kingdom of God."

Apostle Eric L. Warren—Eric Warren Ministries
Charlotte, North Carolina, USA

ESCHATOLOGY – A BIBLICAL VIEW

If you were a time traveler and traveled back to the time of say Abraham Lincoln and told him you were from the future in 21st century. What if he asked you how people communicated in the 21st century, and now you had to try and explain say how an email works. How would you explain it?

Would you use something he would be familiar with to describe it? Perhaps you would tell him that in the future postmen would ride horses at 500 mile per hour. Or you might tell him you could deliver a message by train from New York to LA in less than one day. You're trying to find a way to communicate how

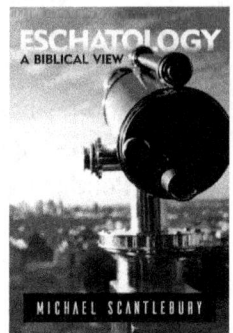

"fast" an email really is. But you're trying to do in a way that wouldn't totally blow his mind.

That's kind of the conundrum we have when trying to understand difficult verses in the Bible, especially in themes like eschatology. The prophetic writers of Scripture had to convey God's mysteries in language that their readers would understand.

Fast forward now 2-3,000 years later, and we are reading these prophetic Scriptures through a 21st century lens, and sometimes coming up with all kinds of weird speculative interpretations because we didn't understand what those Scriptures would have meant to a first century Believer, or a Jew living in the time of the OT Prophets.

The book before you plan to delve deeper into this and much more as it seeks to present you with a sensible view of eschatology.

THE RESTORATION OF ZION

When you hear the word Zion, what comes to mind? As Christians, we've sung the choruses and the hymns about Zion or Mount Zion, but do we fully understand just what we're singing about? Do we know what it is? The Bible promises the full restoration of Zion, and if we don't fully know what Zion is, what then do we anticipate in terms of its restoration?

The greatest hindrance to accurate interpretation and application of Scripture is a futuristic view of Scripture. This futuristic view continues to rob the Believer of experiencing God in His fullness in the here and now.

In this book, we will uncover within the Scriptures exactly what Zion actually represents to the New Testament Believer. So lay down any preconceived ideas you may have, delve into the pages of this book, and let it speak truth to you.

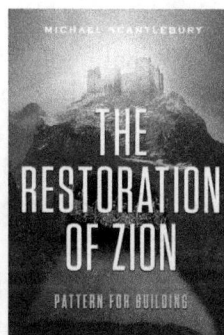

AS IT WAS IN THE BEGINNING SO SHALL IT BE...

Have you ever wondered about life and all of its intricacies? Why are we here on planet earth? What is out there in deep dark space? Who created it all in its majesty and wonder with the brilliancy of everything that surrounds us?

Since time began, man has tried to explain things regarding the known world. One forward thinker put forth a theory that the world was flat. That was refuted by more research. Study and research and pondering some more have revealed some truth about our world but not all the questions are yet answered.

While many of us as Christians enjoy documentaries on the pondering of the many ways we may have "gotten here" beginning with the theory of alien transports dropping us off, to the idea of a cosmic slime pit which one day came to life, so truly the only authority we have as born-again followers of Jesus Christ is the book of Genesis, the very first book of the Holy Scriptures, which simply states: "In the beginning God created the heavens and the earth." Genesis 1:1

We will broach the answers to these and other questions only God's inspired word, the Holy Bible will answer the many questions at hand.

We will begin our journey into the heart and mind of this incredible Creator to learn the reason and purpose for our existence. And as we take that incredible journey, we would seek to come to terms with the revealed, eventual outcome of our existence and life upon planet earth.

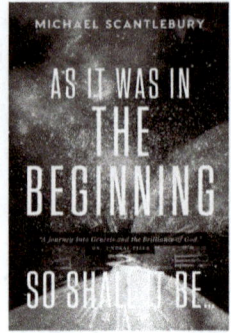

STUDY GUIDE – DANIEL IN BABYLON

This is an exciting study into the present truth lifestyle illustrated through the lives of Daniel and his friends. Whether you'll be meeting with others in a group or going through this book on your own, you've made an excellent decision by choosing to read **DANIEL in Babylon** and studying it in-depth with this guide.

This is a seminal study with strong Apostolic messaging, yet its flowing style allows for easy assimilation of biblical

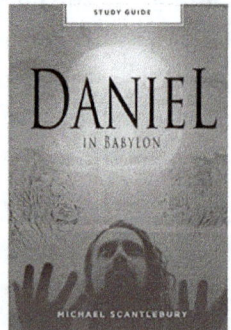

truths, and provides accurate insights for the cerebral Believer, who like Daniel and his companions, are usually the target of the world system. In this book various methodologies are outlined through which, spiritual Babylon seeks to entice the brightest and best of every Godly generation, to acculturize, rob of spiritual identity and manipulate to promote world kingdom end.

PRINCIPLES FOR VICTORIOUS LIVING: VOL II

The initial purpose of the five-fold ministry is for the perfecting or maturing of the Saints, which leads to its next intention, which is the real work of the ministry of Jesus Christ, reconciling the world back to the Father. This book lends itself to help in the maturing of the Saints. It adds insight and strategies that help in achieving exponential personal growth preparing one for the real work of the ministry. This is a volume of information and revelation needed in such a time as this, when maturity and focus are the needed key components that bring us an overcoming victory in this realm and advance the Kingdom of God.

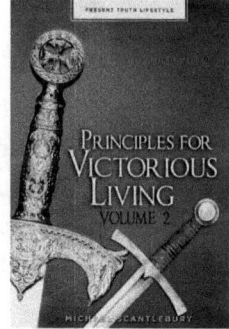

PRINCIPLES FOR VICTORIOUS LIVING: VOL I

The information contained herein is well balanced with a spiritual maturity that keenly stems from wisdom and revelation in the knowledge of Christ. This is the anointing of an Apostle, and the truths that our brother shares will certainly cause you to excel in the Kingdom of God long before this life is over when later we enter the eternals. There's so much to experience today in this life, and Michael extracts so much from the Word of God to facilitate that. His insight of revelation and ability to interpret and articulate what his spirit receives from the Lord are powerful.

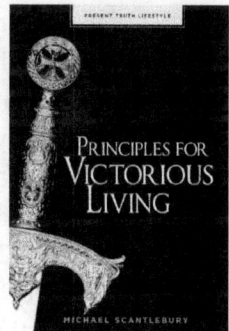

PRESENT TRUTH LIFESTYLE – DANIEL IN BABYLON

This is a seminal study with strong Apostolic messaging, yet its flowing style allows for easy assimilation of biblical truths, and provides accurate insights for the cerebral Believer, who like Daniel and his companions, are usually the target of the world system. In this book various methodologies are outlined through which, spiritual Babylon seeks to entice the brightest and best of every Godly generation, to acculturize, rob of spiritual identity and manipulate to promote world kingdom end.

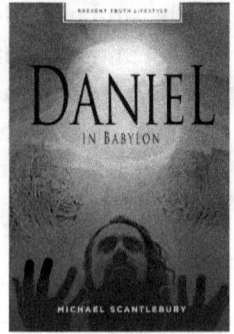

But thanks be to God, there is still a generation in the earth spiritually alert enough to operate within the world system, yet deploy their talents and giftings to bring honour and glory to God. Those with the Daniel mindset will decode dreams and visions and interpret judgements written on the kingdoms of this world in this season.

ESTHER PRESENT TRUTH CHURCH

In a season where the Church co-exists harmoniously with truth and error, this book provides us with a precision tool and well-calibrated instrument of change that is able to fine-tune the global Body of Christ.

The Book of Esther is rich with revelation that is still valid and applicable for the day in which we live. Hidden within its pages is a powerful "present truth" message. The lives of the people involved and the conditions that are seen have spiritual parallels for the Church. Our destiny as the Body of Christ is revealed. The preparations and conditions we must attain to are all similar.

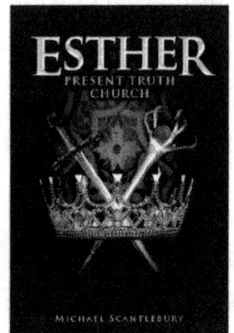

THE FORTRESS CHURCH

According to Webster's English Dictionary "fortress" is defined as: a fortified place: stronghold, *especially*: A large and permanent fortification sometimes including a town. A place that is protected against attack. This book seeks to describe what is a "Fortress Church". We would be looking into the dynamics of this Church as

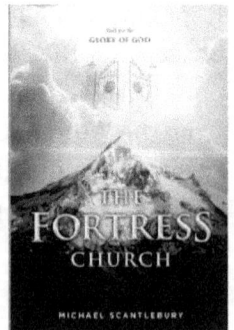

described in Jacob's vision in Genesis Chapter 28, also as described by the Prophet Isaiah, in Isaiah Chapter 2 and as the one detailed in a Psalm of the sons of Korah in Psalms Chapter 48. We would also be looking at a working model of this type of church as found at Antioch in the Book of Acts. Finally we would be exploring The Church at Ephesus, where the Apostle Paul by the Holy Spirit revealed some powerful descriptions of The Church.

CALLED TO BE AN APOSTLE

This autobiography spans fifty-two years of my life on the earth thus far and I have the hope of living several more... Our home was always packed with young people and we did enjoy times of really wonderful fellowship! Although we were experiencing these wonderful times of fellowship my appetite and desire to grow in the things of God continued unabated. I continued to read anything and everything that I could put my hands on that would strengthen my life. I began reading Wigglesworth, Moody, Finney, Idahosa, Lake, and the list went on and on! But the more I read the more this question burned in my heart–"*why is it that every time we hear/read about a move of God, it is always miles away and in another country? Why can't I experience some of the things that I am reading about?*" Little did I know the Lord would answer that desire!

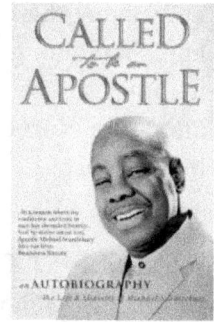

LEAVENED REVEALED

The Bible has a lot to say about *leaven* and its effects upon the Believer. Leaven as an ingredient gives a false sense of growth. In the New Testament there are at least six types of *leaven* spoken about and we will be exploring them in detail, in order to ensure that our lives are completely free of the first five, and completely influenced by the sixth! These types of leaven include the following: The leaven of the Pharisees; The leaven of the Sadducees; The leaven of the Galatians; The leaven of Herod; The leaven of the Corinthians. However, the Leaven of the Kingdom of God is the only type of leaven that has the power and capacity to bring about true growth and lasting change to our lives.

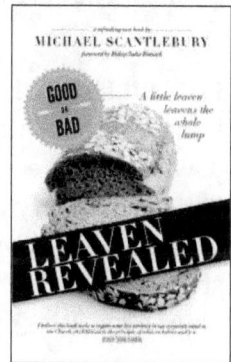

I WILL BUILD MY CHURCH — JESUS CHRIST

"For we are his *masterpiece*, created in Christ Jesus for good works that God prepared long ago to be our way of life." Ephesians 2:10

What a powerful picture of The Church of Jesus Christ–His Masterpiece! Reference to a *masterpiece* lends to the idea that there are other pieces and among them all, this particular one stands head and shoulders above the rest! This is so true when it comes to The Church that Jesus Christ is building; when you place it alongside everything else that God has created, The Church is by far His Masterpiece!

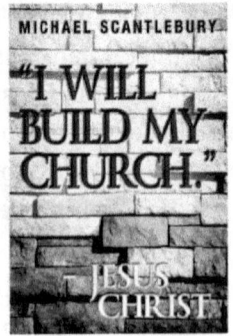

JESUS CHRIST THE APOSTLE AND HIGH PRIEST OF OUR PROFESSION

There is a dimension to the apostolic nature of Jesus Christ that I would like to capture in His one-on-one encounters with several people during the time He walked the face of the earth and functioned as Apostle. In this book we will explore several significant encounters that Jesus Christ had with different people where valuable principles and insight can be gleaned. They are designed to change your life.

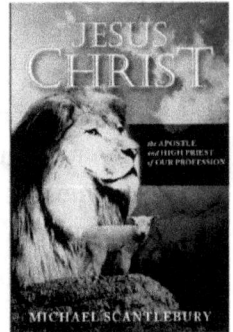

FIVE PILLARS OF THE APOSTOLIC

It has become very evident that a new day has dawned in the earth, as the Lord restores the foundational ministry of the Apostle back to His Church. This book will give you a clear and concise understanding of what the Holy Spirit is doing in The Church today.

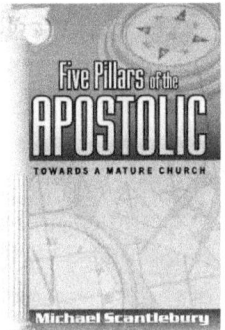

APOSTOLIC PURITY

In every dispensation, in every move of God's Holy Spirit to bring restoration and reformation to His Church, righteousness, holiness and purity has always been of utmost importance to the Lord. This book will challenge your to walk pure as you seek to fulfil God's Will for your life and ministry.

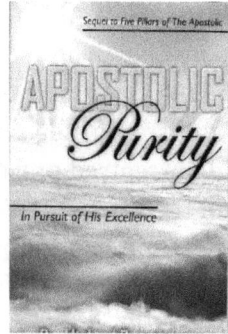

GOD'S NATURE EXPRESSED THROUGH HIS NAMES

How awesome it would be when we encounter God's Nature through the varied expressions of His Names. His Names give us reference and guidance as to how He works towards and in us as His people–and by extension to society! As a matter of fact it adds a whole new meaning to how you draw near to Him; and by this you can now begin to know His Ways because you have come into relationship with His Nature.

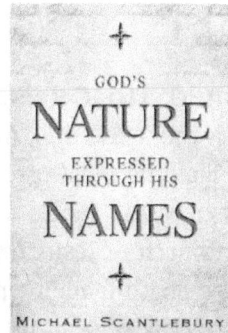

INTERNAL REFORMATION

Internal Reformation is multifaceted. It is an ecclesiology laying out the blue print of The Church Jesus Christ is building in today's world. At the same time it is a manual laying out the modus operandi of how Believers are called to function as dynamic, militant over-comers who are powerful because they carry internally the very character and DNA of Jesus Christ.

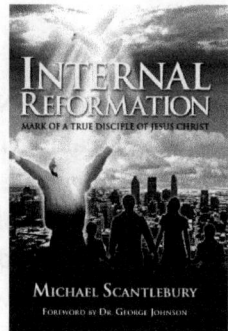

KINGDOM ADVANCING PRAYER VOL I

The Church of Jesus Christ is stronger and much more determined and equipped than she has ever been, and strong, aggressive, powerful, Spirit-Filled, Kingdom-centred prayers are being lifted in every nation in the earth. This kind of prayer is released from the heart of Father God into the hearts of His people, as we seek for His Glory to cover the earth as the waters cover the sea.

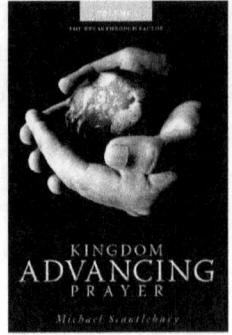

APOSTOLIC REFORMATION

If the axe is dull, And one does not sharpen the edge, Then he must use more strength; But wisdom brings success." (Ecclesiastes 10:10) For centuries The Church of Jesus Christ has been using quite a bit of strength while working with a dull axe (sword, Word of God, revelation), in trying to get the job done. This has been largely due to the fact that she has been functioning without Apostles, the ones who have been graced and anointed by the Lord, with the ability to sharpen.

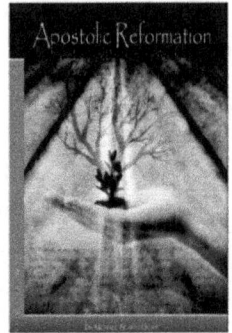

KINGDOM ADVANCING PRAYER VOL II

Prayer is calling for the Bridegroom's return, and for the Bride to be made ready. Prayers are storming the heavens and binding the "strong men" declaring and decreeing God's Kingdom rule in every jurisdiction. This is what we call Kingdom Advancing Prayer. What a *Glorious Day* to be *Alive* and to be in the *Will* and *Plan of Father God*! *Hallelujah*!

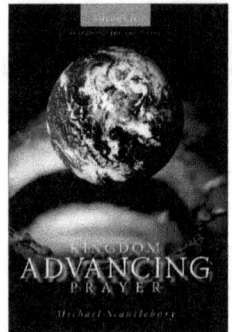

KINGDOM ADVANCING PRAYER VOLUME III

One of the keys to the amazing rise to greater functionality of The Church is the clear understanding of what we call Kingdom Advancing Prayer. This kind of prayer reaches into the very core of the demonic stronghold and destroys demonic kings and princes and establishes the Kingdom and Purpose of the Lord. This is the kind of prayer that Jesus Christ engaged in, to bring to pass the will of His Father while He was upon planet earth.

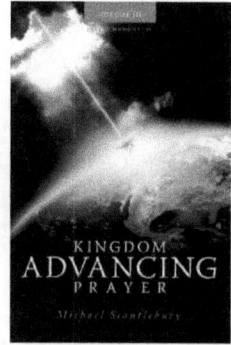

www.ingramcontent.com/pod-product-compliance
Lightning Source LLC
LaVergne TN
LVHW021347080426
835508LV00020B/2150